BETTER THAN LIFE

BETTER THAN LIFE

Daniel Pennac

Translated by David Homel

Coach House Press
Toronto

Coach House Press
50 Prince Arthur Avenue, Suite 107
Toronto, Canada M5R 1B5

© Coach House Press, 1994
First published as *Comme un Roman* by Editions Gallimard in 1992
© Editions Gallimard, 1992
English Translation © David Homel, 1994

Editor for the Press: Alberto Manguel

FIRST EDITION
Printed in Canada

Canadian Cataloguing in Publication Data

Pennac, Daniel
Better than Life
Translation of: Comme un roman.
ISBN 0-88910-484-0
1. Books and reading. 2. Literature – Study and teaching.
3. Reading interests. I. Title
Z1003.C613 1994   028'.9   C94-931751-9

For Franklin Rist,
a great reader of novels
and a character himself

In memory of my father,
and in daily remembrance
of Frank Vlieghe

CONTENTS

Translator's Note: The use of the masculine pronoun "he" is not meant to exclude female readers who, as we all know, buy and read more books than men do.

~ ONE ~

THE BIRTH OF AN ALCHEMIST

1

You can't make people read. Any more than you can make them love, or dream.

Mind you, you can always try. Go ahead. "Love me!" "Dream!" "Read!" "Read, I said, for Christ's sake, I'm ordering you to read!"

"Go up to your room and read!"

The result?

Utter failure.

He's fallen asleep over his book. He's flown, out the window, into a world so much more desirable than the one in the pages. He's escaped from his reading. But he's posted a sentry: the book is still open under his cheek. Walk into his bedroom and there he is, sitting at his desk, diligently reading. Even if we sneak up on him, he'll hear us coming from the surface of his sleep.

"Is it good?"

He'd never say no. That would be treason. Books are sacred. How can anyone not like to read? No, he'll just tell us that, well, the descriptions do go on a little too long.

Reassured, we return to our television set. Though his comment might set off a passionate debate between us and our near-and-dear.

"He thinks the descriptions go on too long. What do you expect, this is the visual age. In the nineteenth century, writers had to describe everything."

"That's no reason to let him skip half the pages!"

There's no rebuttal.

Why bother? Upstairs, the century's child has already gone back to sleep.

2

How can we ever understand his aversion to reading if we came from a generation, an era, a background, a family where the norm was to prevent us from reading?

"Stop reading, will you, you'll ruin your eyes!"

"Go out and play instead, it's a nice day."

"Turn off the light, it's late!"

The day was always too nice for reading, and the night too dark.

To read or not to read, the verb was always used in the imperative. Things haven't changed. Back then, reading was a subversive act. The discovery of the novel went hand-in-hand with the excitement of disobedience. Doubly splendid! How sweet the memory of those stolen hours of reading underneath the covers with a flashlight, while Anna Karenina galloped breathlessly through the night towards her Vronsky! Those two loved each other, and that was good, but what was even better, they loved each other in defiance of the ban on reading! Their love defied Mother and Father, their love defied the math homework that had to be finished, the English essay that had to be turned in, the room that had to be cleaned up, their love was better than dessert, they preferred each other to a ball game or berry-picking. They had chosen each other and preferred each other to everything else ... What love could be better?

Only, the novel was too short.

3

To be fair, we didn't turn reading into an obligation right away. At first, we were thinking only of his pleasure. His early years had put us in a state of grace. The absolute wonder of this new life endowed us with a kind of genius. For him, we became storytellers. As soon as he could understand language, we told him stories. We didn't even know we had that skill. His pleasure inspired us. His happiness made us inventive. For him, we created characters, added on the chapters, refined the suspense ... The way old Tolkien did for his grandchildren, we invented a world for him. As day slipped into night, we became his novelist.

If we'd had no talent for storytelling, we would have told him other people's stories and probably told them poorly, grasping for words, mispronouncing the names, confusing the chapters, grafting the beginning of one story onto the end of another ... Even if we'd told no stories at all and settled for reading out loud, we still would have been his novelist, the storyteller thanks to whom, every evening, he slipped into his dream pyjamas and stretched out under the covers of the night. Better yet, we were the Book.

Remember that togetherness. It has no equal.

How we loved to frighten him for the sheer pleasure of reassuring him! How he demanded that fear from us! Already so skeptical, yet trembling just a bit. A perfect reader, in other words. That was how our relationship worked in those days. He, the reader, with his cleverness, and we, the book, willing accomplices!

4

We taught him about books before he knew how to read. We opened his mind to the infinite diversity of the imagination, we initiated him into the joys of arm-chair travel, we gave him the gift of being everywhere at once, we saved him from Chronos, we bestowed upon him the fabulous solitude of the reader ... The stories we read to him teemed with brothers, sisters, parents, doubles, hosts of guardian angels and tute-lary friends who took charge of his fears but who, when fighting their own ogres, found a haven in the anxious beating of his heart. He became their recip-rocal angel: a reader. Without him, their world would not have existed. Without them, he would have remained mired in the heaviness of his own. He dis-covered the paradoxical virtue of reading: it takes us out of the world so we may find meaning in it.

He returned silent from those travels. It was morning, we had other things on our mind. And to tell the truth, we didn't ask what he had learned on the other side. Innocently, he nurtured that mystery. His private relations with Snow White or one of the Seven Dwarfs were confidential, demanding secrecy. For a reader, one of life's pleasures is the silence after the book.

Yes, we taught him all about books.

And whet his reader's appetite.

Remember? Back then, *he couldn't wait to learn how to read!*

5

What teachers we were, when we had no concern
with teaching!

6

Now he is a reclusive adolescent in his room, faced with a book he cannot read. His desire to be elsewhere creates a smeary film between his eyes and the page. He is sitting in front of the window, the door closed behind him. Stuck on page 48. He can't bear to count the hours it took him just to get to this forty-eighth page. The book has exactly 446 of them. Might as well say 500. Five hundred pages! If only there were dialogue. No such luck! Pages stuffed with crowded lines between two narrow margins, dark paragraphs balancing one on top of the other with, now and again, the meager charity of a line of speech. A set of quotation marks like an oasis: one character is speaking to another. But the second character doesn't answer. Here comes another twelve-page block! A dozen pages of black ink! It's suffocating! Like being at the bottom of a mineshaft! Damn it! he swears. Sorry, but he does swear. Damned impossible book! Page 48 ... If only he could remember what happened on the previous forty-seven pages! He can't bear to consider that question, but it's the one he'll be asked, for sure. Winter night has fallen. From the depths of the house, the theme announcing the TV news reaches his ears. Another half hour to use up before dinner. A book is an extremely dense object. It gives you no way in. It doesn't even burn very well. Fire can't slip between its pages. Not enough air in there. Marginal notes he makes for himself. And his margins are enormous. A book is thick, compact, dense, it's a blunt instrument. Page 48 or page 148, what's the difference? The view is the same. He pictures the teacher's lips pronouncing the book's title. And hears the question his friends ask in unison.

"How many pages?"

"Three or four hundred."

(Lies!)

"When's it due?"

When the fateful day is named, it sets off a storm of protest.

"Two weeks? Four hundred pages (500, really) of reading in two weeks? But, sir, we could never do that!"

There's no negotiating with this teacher.

A book is a blunt instrument, a block of eternity. The material manifestation of boredom. It's a book. The Book. That's what he calls it in all his papers: the book, a book, all books, some books.

"In his book on reason, Descartes tells us that ..."

The teacher protests in vain: *book* is not the correct term of reference. One must speak of a novel, an essay, a short-story collection, a volume of poetry, the word book in itself, in its ability to designate anything at all ends up saying nothing in particular, a telephone book is a book, so is a dictionary, a restaurant guide, a stamp collection, a list of accounts payable ...

It's no use. In his next paper, the word springs spontaneously from his pen.

"In his book, *A Tale of Two Cities,* Dickens tells us that ..."

From the point of view of his current solitude, a book is a book is a book. And every book weighs as much as an encyclopedia, one of those hard-backed volumes slipped under his rear end as a boy, so he could reach the level of the dinner table.

A book's weight drags you down. A moment ago, he was sitting in relative lightness on his chair, with all the buoyancy of good intentions. But after a few pages, he began to feel overwhelmed by that unfortunately familiar heaviness, the weight of the book, the weight of boredom, the intolerable burden of fruitless effort.

His eyelids announced the imminent shipwreck.

The reef of page 48 opened a breach beneath the water-line of his good intentions.

The book pulled him under.

They sank to the bottom together.

7

Meanwhile, downstairs, in front of the set, the argument over the corrupting effects of television has won two new converts.

"The stupidity, the vulgarity, the violence of those programs ... It's incredible! You can't turn on the TV without seeing it."

"Those combat cartoons are the worst. Have you ever looked at one of those violent cartoons?"

"It's not just the programs. It's television itself. The superficiality, and how passive the viewer is."

"You turn it on, you sit down ..."

"You jump from channel to channel ..."

"Your attention span is ruined ..."

"At least you can skip the ads."

"Not anymore. They've developed synchronized

programming. You escape from one ad and run into another."

"Sometimes the same one!"

Silence falls. We've identified an area of agreement. We're dazzled by the blinding radiance of our adult lucidity.

Then, *mezza voce,* we speak.

"Now, reading, obviously, reading is different, it's a conscious act!"

"That's exactly right, that's what I was thinking, reading is an act, 'the act of reading,' that's very true ..."

"Whereas with television, or even the movies, when you think about it, everything is provided for you, nothing has to be made new, everything's been pre-consumed, the image, the sound, the sets, the soundtrack in case you didn't figure out what the director wants you to feel ..."

"The door squeaking open to remind you it's time to get scared ..."

"When you read, you have to *imagine* all those things. Reading is an act of constant creation."

Another silence.

Between two parents. Two creators.

Then these words.

"What bothers me most is the number of hours an average kid spends watching TV, compared to the time he spends in English class. I've read statistics about it."

"It must be incredible!"

"One hour for every six or seven. Plus time spent at the movies. A child—I'm not talking about ours—spends an average, a minimum, of two hours a day in front of a television set, and eight to ten hours during the weekend. That adds up to thirty-six hours, compared to just five a week for English."

"No wonder our schools are fighting a losing battle."

A third silence falls.

It makes us think of a bottomless pit.

8

Evening. A dinner party among creators like us.

There were any number of things, really, we could have said to describe the distance between him and books.

Of course, we said them all.

That television is not the only culprit.

That between our children's generation and ours, each decade is as long as a century.

That even if we feel psychologically closer to our children than our parents did to us, intellectually speaking, we still reflect our parents.

(Here, controversy and discussion break out around the dinner table. The adverbs "psychologically" and "intellectually" are redefined. A new adverb is brought in as reinforcement.)

"*Affectively* closer, if you like."

"Effectively?"

"I didn't say effectively, I said *affectively*."

"In other words, we're affectively closer to our children, but effectively closer to our parents. Is that it?"

"I'm talking about social facts. A complex of social facts with these results: our children are also the sons and daughters of their own times, whereas we were only the children of our parents."

"Whatever do you mean by that?"

"It's simple! As adolescents, we weren't consumers of our society. Commercially, culturally, we inhabited adult society. Shared clothing, shared food, shared culture, the little brother inherited the shirts and pants of the older brother, we all ate the same things, at the same time, at the same table, we went on the same Sunday excursions, the television bound the family together with a channel or two (much better ones, by the way, than the plethora of choices we have now), and as far as reading was concerned, our parents' only thought was to put certain titles on the top shelf where we couldn't get at them."

"As for our grandparents' generation, they simply refused to let girls read."

"True enough. Especially novels. Too much imagination is not a good thing. It doesn't make for happy marriages ..."

"Whereas, these days, teenagers are full-fledged consumers of a society that dresses them, entertains them and cultivates them. A society of McDonald's, Reeboks and Chicago Bulls T-shirts. We went to surprise parties; they go to raves. We read books; they listen to tapes. We communicated through the Beatles; they lurk behind the autism of the Walkman. Nowadays, there's an entirely brand-new phenomenon: whole city blocks taken over by adolescence, vast urban and suburban territories devoted to adolescent rage and confusion."

Here, the dreadful shopping mall is conjured up.

The seat of all evils.

The mall, city or suburban, teeming with fantasies, hanging out, sex-and-drugs-and-rock-'n'-roll, subterranean adolescent life!

The illiterate hordes with their first-grade sentence structures, a society of swarmers!

Silence settles over the dinner table again. The silence of pins dropping.

"Do your kids hang out at the mall?"

"No. Luckily, there's not one nearby."
Silence.
All is silence.
"In other words, they've stopped reading."
"That's right."
"Distracted by too many other things."
"Yes."

9

And if it's not television's fault or the consumer society's doing, then it must be the electronic invasion. And if it's not the fault of those hypnotic little games, then it's school itself: the total lack of reading and writing skills, the outdated programs, the incompetence of the teachers, the lamentable state of the classrooms, the threadbare libraries.

Let's see, what have we forgotten?

Oh, yes, the cutbacks at the Department of Education: a scandal! And, in that microscopic budgetary envelope, the infinitesimal amount for books.

Under those conditions, how do you expect my son, my daughter, our children, all young people, to read?

"Besides, society in general is reading less."

"True enough."

10

And so our arguments run, the eternal victory of language over the opacity of things, luminous silences that reveal more than they hide. We are vigilant and well informed; society cannot fool us. We define the world with our words, though real illumination comes from what we don't say. We are lucid. Better yet—we have a passion for lucidity.

So why do we feel this vague, post-party sadness? This midnight silence in the house that has recovered its solitude? Is it not more than the prospect of the dishes that remain undone? A few miles away, at a traffic light, in the cocoon of their car, our friends are mired in the same silence that pounces on couples returning from their night out. The intoxication of lucidity fades, leaving a taste like that of sour drunkenness, the anesthesia wearing off, the slow swimming upward towards consciousness, the return to oneself, and the vaguely painful feeling of not having recognized ourselves in the things we said. *We just weren't there.* Everything else was in its proper place, our points were well argued, and as far as we were concerned, we had truth on our side. But we just weren't there. Another evening sacrificed to the numbing practice of lucidity.

That's how it is. You think your words have seized the problem, whereas the problem has seized your words.

The things we said back there at the dinner table were totally out of synch with our inner voice. We were discussing the necessity of reading, but secretly we were at his side, upstairs, in his room, where he was not reading. We were listing all the good reasons the current age gave him for not reading, but all the while we were searching for a way to break through the wall of books that separates him from us. We were talking about books, whereas our thoughts were with him.

He really didn't help things by coming into the dining room at the last minute, plopping down his adolescent awkwardness without the least grunt of hello, making no effort to participate in the conversation and, finally, leaving the table before dessert was served.

"Sorry, but there's something I've got to read!"

II

Togetherness lost ...

Insomnia settles in as we remember the evening ritual of reading at the foot of his bed, when he was small, always the same time, the same preparations. It was a little like praying. A sudden state of grace after the uproar of the day, a coming together that healed life's little wounds, the ceremonial moment of silence before the first words of the tale were spoken, our voice finally ringing true, the liturgy of chapters ... Yes, reading a story every evening fulfilled the finest function of prayer, the most impartial, the least speculative, the one that touches only the human kind: the forgiveness of trespasses. No wrongdoing was confessed, we weren't grasping for our portion of eternity, it was a moment of communion, the absolution of the text, a return to the only paradise worthy of the name: togetherness. Without realizing it, we were discovering one of the essential functions of stories—and more than that, of art itself—which is to call a truce in the daily battle we fight.

Love was given new skin.

Everything was freely bestowed.

12

Free. That's how he understood it. A gift. A time out of time. Set against the world outside. The nightly story freed him from the weight of the day. He cast off, he went with the wind, almost weightless, and the wind was our voice.

No fare was asked of him for this journey, not a penny. He need give nothing in return. It wasn't even a reward. (Rewards! As if you had to be worthy to receive a reward!) Here, the greatest treasures were given free of charge.

For freedom is the only currency of art.

13

Tell me, then, what happened between those scenes of togetherness and the way he is now, struggling to scale the heights of a book, as we attempt to understand him (that is, to reassure ourselves) by blaming the century and its television set which, incidentally, we might have neglected to turn off.

Television's fault?

Is the twentieth century too visual, the nineteenth too descriptive? Then wouldn't the eighteenth be too rational, the seventeenth too classical, the sixteenth too Renaissance, Pushkin too Russian and Sophocles too dead? As if the relations between people and books dissolved only after centuries of misunderstanding.

Actually, a few years was all it took.

A few weeks.

The misunderstanding began.

At the foot of his bed, we used to conjure up Little Red Riding Hood's red cloak and the contents of her basket in the most minute detail, not to mention the darkness of the forest, and the grand-mother's ears that turned out to be much too hairy, and every flower along the path. Funny, but I never remember him complaining that our descriptions were too long.

There's no sense blaming the passage of time. Life itself is at fault, *our* lives, the way we hammer away at sacred principles like this one: *"You must read."*

14

What is our life but the erosion of pleasure? A year full of stories at his bedside, yes. Two years, all right. Three, if you insist. That adds up to one thousand and ninety-five stories, at the rate of one per evening. Quite a figure! And then, our efforts went far beyond the fifteen minutes of storytelling. We had to take the time to choose the gift. What story can I possibly tell him tonight? What can I read to him next?

We were running out of inspiration.

At first, he helped out. The magic he demanded wasn't contained in any story, but in *the* story.

"Tom Thumb! I want Tom Thumb again!"

"There are other stories besides Tom Thumb, honey, there's ..."

It was Tom Thumb or nothing.

Who would have thought we would long for those happy days when Tom Thumb, and Tom Thumb alone, filled his enchanted forest? Why did we ever open new books for him and let him choose among them?

"No, not that one, you already read me that one!"

Though it never reached the level of obsession, the problem of choice certainly was a headache. Full of brief good intentions, we promised we'd go to a bookstore the next Saturday in search of children's literature. The next Saturday, we put it off to the Saturday after. What was for him a period of sacred waiting became part of our domestic routine. A small errand, but an errand nevertheless, added to the pile of more important ones. Small or not, a pleasure reduced to the status of an errand should have set alarm bells ringing. We didn't listen to their clamor.

Sometimes we rebelled against the responsibility.

"Why me? Why not you? Sorry, but tonight you're telling him his story!"

"You know I don't have the imagination for that kind of thing."

Whenever the occasion arose, we sent a surrogate

voice to his bedside. A cousin, a babysitter, an aunt who happened to be in town, a voice that had not yet been pressed into service, and still found the exercise charming. But the owner of that voice often sang a different tune when the audience turned out to be too demanding.

"That's not what the grandmother says!"

We schemed shamefully, too. We knew how much he valued his story, and considered using it as blackmail.

"If you don't calm down, there'll be no story tonight!"

Rarely did we make good on our threats. Bawling him out or taking away his dessert were ordinary punishments. But to send him to bed without a story was like casting his day into utter darkness. Leaving him without our moment of communion. The punishment would have been intolerable for both of us.

It's true, we used the threat, oh, no more than a few times. It was a careless expression of our weariness, the shameful desire to use, just this once, those fifteen minutes for something else, for cleaning up the house, or a moment of silence ...

or to do a little reading ourselves.

The storyteller in us was exhausted. Ready to pass on the torch.

15

School came just in time.

It took responsibility for the future.

Reading, writing, arithmetic.

At the beginning, he went at it with real enthusiasm.

How amazing that those tails and circles and little bridges joined together formed real letters! And that those letters could make syllables, and those syllables, one after the other, words. He couldn't believe it. And that some of those words were familiar to him—it was magical!

Mommy, for example, *mommy,* three little bridges, a circle, then three more little bridges done twice, then two slanting sticks, and the result was *mommy.* How could such a wonder ever cease to amaze him?

Try to picture the moment. He got up early. He was with his mother, the one whose name he would soon be writing, he went out into the autumn drizzle (yes, an autumn drizzle, the light was the color of an uncleaned aquarium, let's not skimp on the dramatic details), he headed for the school still wrapped in the warmth of his bed, the taste of cereal in his mouth, tightly holding the hand just above his head, walking as quickly as he could, taking two steps for his mother's one, his little knapsack bouncing on his back, then came the school door, the rapid kiss goodbye, the asphalt playground with its row of maples, the clanging bell ... at first he took shelter from the rain under the overhang, then he joined the schoolyard games, but a few minutes later they all found themselves sitting behind Lilliputian desks, quiet and no moving around, all the body's movements concentrated on the effort of moving the pencil down this low-ceilinged corridor called the line. Tongue stuck out, fingers numb and wrist stiff ... little bridges, circles, tails, sticks, more little bridges ... he is miles from his mother now, lost in this strange solitude called *effort,* in the company of all those other solitudes with their tongues stuck out ... and now the first letters are assembled ... lines of "a's," lines of "m's," of "q's" (the "q" is no joke with its diving, backwards tail, but it's a piece of cake compared to the "s" with its treacherous curves, and the "k" with its spray of lines shooting out every which way), all the difficult ones conquered so that, little by little, as if they were magnetized, the letters come together spontaneously into syllables, lines of *mom* and *dad,* and the syllables in turn making words ...

Then, one day, his ears still humming from the commotion of the lunchroom, he contemplated the silent flowering of the word on white paper, there, before his eyes: *mommy.*

He'd seen it on the blackboard, of course, and recognized it, but now, right here, he had written it with his own hand.

In a voice that quavered at first, he stumbled over the two syllables, separately. "Mom-my."

Then, suddenly, he understood.

"Mommy!"

His triumphant cry celebrated the culmination of the greatest intellectual voyage ever, a sort of first step on the moon, the movement from an arbitrary set of lines to the most emotionally charged meaning. Little bridges, circles and slanting sticks ... and you could say "Mommy!" There it was, written, right there, and he had done it! Not a combination of syllables, not a word or a concept anymore. It wasn't *any* mother, it was *his* mother, a magical transformation, infinitely more eloquent than the most faithful photographic likeness, built from nothing but little circles and sticks and bridges, that have now suddenly—and forever!—become more than scratches on paper. They have become her presence, her voice, the good way she smelled this morning, her lap, that infinity of details, that wholeness, so intimately absolute, and so absolutely foreign to what is written there, on the rails of the page, within the four walls of the classroom.

Lead into gold.

Nothing less.

He had just turned lead into gold.

16

You never get over that transformation. You don't return from a voyage like that unchanged. No matter how inhibited, the *pleasure of reading* presides over every act of reading. By its nature, its alchemical sensuality, the pleasure of reading has no fear of visual media, not even the daily avalanche of pictures on the TV screen.

Even if the pleasure of reading has been lost (which is what we mean when we say that my son, my daughter, young people today, don't like reading), it hasn't gone very far.

It's just under the surface.

Easily found.

We simply need to know where to look. To focus our search, we should state a few home truths that have nothing to do with the effect of the modern world on today's youth. A few truths that concern only us. We who say we love reading and who claim we want to share that love.

17

He comes home from school, still under the spell of this magic, proud of himself, happy. He displays his ink-stains as if they were medals. The spiderwebs of his four-color ballpoint are a badge of pride.

His happiness is compensation for the tortures of grade school: the absurdly long days, the teacher's demands, the steamy lunchroom, his nervous stomach.

He returns home, opens his bag, displays his prowess, reproduces his sacred words. *Mommy* or *daddy*, *dog* or *cat*, or his own name.

Overnight, he has become the tireless pitchman for the great epistle of advertising. TOYOTA. COKE. DELTA. NIKE. Giant words falling out of the sky, their colorful syllables exploding from his mouth. Not a single brand of laundry detergent can resist his passion for decoding.

"'Whi-ter-whites.' What's 'whiterwhites' mean?"

The time has come to answer the basic questions.

18

Were we blinded by his enthusiasm? Did we believe that, as long as a child took pleasure in words, he would naturally be drawn to books? Did we think that learning to read was an innate process, like walking or talking—just another privilege of our species? Whatever the reason, we decided to put an end to our bedtime stories.

School was teaching him how to read, he took to his lessons with real enthusiasm, it was a turning-point in his life, a new autonomy, a second version of his first step. That's what we told ourselves in our own inarticulate way, without ever saying it out loud, so natural did the process seem, as if it were another step in his smooth evolution.

He was grown up now, he could read by himself

and find his way in the realm of signs.

He finally gave us back our fifteen minutes of freedom.

His new-found pride made it easier. He climbed into bed, opened up *Curious George* and propped the book against his knees, a wrinkle of furious concentration between his eyes. *He was reading.*

We would leave his room, believing in his pantomime, without understanding—or wanting to admit—that what a child learns first is not the act but the imitation of the act. The imitation can help in learning; but what it really does is reassure him, by pleasing us.

19

Not that we were negligent parents. We didn't abandon him to the school system. On the contrary: we followed his progress every step of the way. The teacher knew us as concerned parents who attended every meeting and were always "open to dialogue."

We helped him with his homework. And when he exhibited the first signs of reading fatigue, we insisted he do his daily page, out loud, and that he understand its meaning.

That wasn't always easy.

Every syllable was like giving birth.

The meaning of the word was often lost in the effort to pronounce it.

The meaning of the sentence was scattered by the number of words.

Return to the first line.

Begin again.

Endlessly.

"So, what did you just read? What does it mean?"

We usually chose the worst time of the day. When he returned from school, or we, from work. At the height of his fatigue or at the lowest point of our energy.

"You're not trying!"

Irritation, crying, pyrotechnical refusals, slamming doors, stubbornness.

"We'll have to start over again, we'll just have to start over from the beginning!"

And he did, he started over, from the beginning, every word twisted by the trembling of his lips.

"Cut the comedy!"

But his grief was no act. It was real and uncontrollable, it spoke of the pain of losing control, of no longer being able to play his role to our satisfaction. Our concern, more than any outward display of impatience, is what fed his grief.

Because we *were* concerned.

We began comparing him to other children his age.

And questioning our friends whose daughter was doing very well at school, yes, and who absolutely adored reading, yes again.

Did he have a hearing problem? Dyslexic, perhaps? Was he going to turn into a "problem student"? Flunk out of grade school?

Off to the specialists for consultation. His hearing test yielded perfectly normal results. The speech therapists were reassuring. The psychologists, serene.

So?

Was it laziness?

Sheer, ordinary laziness?

No, he was moving at his own speed, that's all. Which was not necessarily anybody else's speed. And which would not necessarily remain constant all his life. His progress as a learning reader had its leaps forward and its sudden retreats, its periods of hunger and its long doldrums with no appetite, its thirst for progress and its fear of disappointing.

The problem is that we teachers are hurried usurers, lending out the knowledge we possess and charging interest. It has to show a profit, and the quicker the better! If not, we might start losing faith in our own methods.

20

If it's true what they say, that my son, my daughter, young people in general, don't love to read—and *love* is the right word, because here we're speaking of a romance that failed—then there's no sense blaming television, or modern life or the school system. If it makes us feel better, all right, let's blame those supposedly guilty parties, but not until we've asked ourselves the basic question. What did we do to the ideal reader our child was in those days when we were both the tale and the teller?

Imagine the betrayal!

The three of us—the child, the story and the parents—formed a Trinity that was reunited each evening. Now he is alone, faced with a hostile book.

The lightness of our words freed him from his

burdens. The mysterious tangle of letters started him dreaming.

We showed him how to stand up straight, but the sheer weight of his effort brought him crashing down.

We let him travel through books. Now he is a prisoner of his room, his school, his book, a sentence, a word.

Where are those magical characters hiding, those brothers and sisters, kings and queens; those heroes, tormented by villains, who freed him from his daily cares by calling upon his help? Could they actually have any relation to those squashed flat ink-spots called letters? Could those demi-gods have crumbled that badly and been reduced to signs on a page? How did books become objects? A curious metamorphosis: magic working backwards towards banality. He and his heroes asphyxiated together in the mute thickness of books.

As a metamorphosis, even that wasn't much compared to his parents' insistence—and his teacher's, too—that he surrender the stronghold of his imagination.

"So, then, what happened to the prince next? Tell me!"

Funny, but his parents never used to worry about whether he had *really* understood that Sleeping Beauty fell asleep in the forest because she'd pricked her finger on the spindle, and Snow White because she'd bitten into the poison apple. (Besides, the first few times, he hadn't really understood, not really. There was so much wonderment in the stories, so many fine words and emotions. All his attention was spent waiting for his favorite passage, and he recited it to himself when the time came. Then came others, more obscure, where all mysteries tangled into a knot, but little by little he understood everything, absolutely everything, he knew that Sleeping Beauty slept because of the spindle, and with Snow White, it was the apple's fault.)

"I'll repeat the question. What happened to the prince when his father drove him from the castle?"

We insist, we push. Good Lord, it's impossible for the kid not to have understood the meaning of a dozen lines! A dozen lines isn't the end of the world!

First, we were his storyteller. Later, we became his accountant.

"If that's the way you want it, you can forget about TV this evening!"

Of course!

Television is lifted to the status of reward. And reading degraded till it becomes a chore. We devised that little system ourselves.

21

Reading is the curse of childhood, yet it is almost the only occupation you can find for children ... A child has no great wish to perfect himself in the use of an instrument of torture, but make it a means to his pleasure, and soon you will not be able to keep him from it.

People make a great fuss about discovering the best way to teach children to read. They invent "bureaux" and cards, they turn the nursery into a printer's shop ... And the pity of it! There is a better way than any of those, and one which is generally overlooked—it consists in the desire to learn. Arouse this desire in your scholar and have done with your "bureaux." ... Any method will serve.

Present interest, that is the motive power, the

only motive power that takes us far and safely.

. . .

I will just add a few words which contain a principle of great importance. It is this—What we are in no hurry to get is usually obtained with speed and certainty.

Okay, okay, Jean-Jacques Rousseau should keep his opinions to himself. After all, he threw out his babies with the family bathwater! (Or so runs the idiotic refrain.)

All the same, he's worth listening to. He reminds us that the adult obsession with "knowing how to read" has been with us for awhile ... as has the stupidity of the various pedagogical gimmicks designed to squash the desire to learn.

As it turns out (do we hear the cynics scoff?), a bad father can have excellent ideas about education, and a good pedagogue can have terrible ones. Life is like that.

But if Rousseau must be struck from the record, what about Paul Valéry—a Frenchman with no interest in the public-welfare system—who, when giving a speech to the young ladies of the austere

Légion d'honneur, a speech both edifying and respectful of scholarly institutions, got right to the point of love, the love of books.

Young ladies, it is by no means through vocabulary and syntax that Literature first begins to seduce us. Seek back through memory and recall how Letters entered your life. In your most tender years, scarcely had your parents stopped singing the lullabies that make newborns smile and send them off to sleep, than the time of stories began. The child drinks them in as he drinks his milk. He demands the next chapter, he insists that the wonders be repeated; he is a pitiless, excellent audience. God knows how many hours I've spent slaking the thirst of children for magicians and monsters, pirates and fairies. And in the end they cry out "More!" to their exhausted father.

22

"He is a pitiless, excellent audience."

He was a good reader from the start. And a good reader he'll remain if the adults in his entourage reward his enthusiasm instead of trying to prove their prowess at his expense. If they stimulate his desire to learn before making him stand up and recite. Accompany him in his efforts instead of waiting for him at the next turning-point. Agree to spend those evenings with him instead of slipping out of his room. Make the present sing instead of threatening him with the future. Refuse to transform what was a pleasure into a chore. Maintain that pleasure until it becomes his, too. Focus on the fact that all cultural learning is free, so they themselves rediscover their own pleasure in this freedom.

23

That pleasure is close by. Easily discovered. It's important not to let too many years go by. We will wait for nightfall, then open the door to his room again, sit down at his bedside and resume our shared reading.

Read.

Out loud.

For the sheer pleasure of it.

His favorite stories.

The results bear describing. At first, he may not believe his ears. The once-burned ear fears the tale. He is on the look-out for a trap, his covers pulled up to his chin.

"Tell me, what did I just read? Did you understand?"

We won't ask him those questions. Those, or any others. We're happy just to read. Freely. Little by little, he relaxes. So do we. Slowly, he begins to recover the dreamy concentration of his evening face. In the end, he will recognize us by our voices, free of anxiety.

He might even fall asleep after the first few minutes, out of sheer relief.

The next evening, the same reunion. And the same pages, probably. Chances are he'll ask us for the same story, just to prove to himself that he hadn't been dreaming. He might even ask us the same questions, at the same spots, for the pleasure of hearing us give him the same answers. Repetition is reassuring. It is proof of togetherness.

He needs to make that demand again: "More!"

In essence, "More, more!" means this: "We must really love each other, mustn't we, to be satisfied with this one story we keep telling over and over again!" To reread is not necessarily to repeat. To reread is to provide fresh proof of enduring love.

And, so, we reread.

His day is behind him. We are here, together at last, *elsewhere* at last. He has rediscovered the mystery of the Trinity: he, the tale and us (in any order you like, for the happiness flows from not having to arrange the elements of this union).

He may treat himself to the ultimate pleasure of the reader, which is to grow weary of the story, then ask us to move onto another.

How many evenings did we spend unlocking the doors of his imagination? Not many. We swore we'd do better. It's worth the trouble, for now we have opened him to all stories.

School goes grinding on with its learning process. If he doesn't immediately show progress in the parroting of his lessons, don't be alarmed. Time is on our side, now that we've stopped trying to make him catch up to it.

Progress, sought-after progress, will show itself in some other area, unexpectedly.

One evening, because we skipped a line, we'll hear him protest.

"You missed something!"

"Excuse me?"

"You didn't read something, you skipped a line!"

"No, how could I ..."

"Give me the book!"

He will grab the book from our hands, and with a triumphant finger, point to the skipped line. *Which he will read out loud.*

That will be our first indication.

Others will follow. Soon he'll make a habit of interrupting our reading.

"How do you write that?"

"What?"

"Prehistoric."

"P.R.E ..."

"Show me!"

But let's not kid ourselves. His sudden wave of curiosity owes something to his new career as an alchemist—but mostly it's a ploy to keep the light on.

So let's not turn it off.

Then, one evening, he will issue a decree.

"I'm reading with you!"

He'll look over our shoulder, and his eyes will follow the lines we read to him.

Then, another step.

"Let me start!"

He prepares to do battle with the first paragraph.

Of course, his reading is laborious at first, and he tires easily. But that doesn't matter: he's regained his confidence, he's reading without fear. He'll volunteer more and more often, with better results each time.

"Tonight, it's my turn!"

He'll choose the same paragraph, of course—the virtues of repetition—then another, his favorite part, then whole stories. Stories he practically knows by heart, that he recognizes more than reads, but that he reads anyway for the pleasure of recognition. Soon will come a time when we discover him, in the morning or the afternoon, with *Winnie-the-Pooh* in hand, reading about the adventures of Eeyore and Piglet and Pooh himself.

Not long ago, he was amazed when he discovered *mommy*. Now, entire stories emerge from the whirlwind of words. He is the hero of his reading, the reader whom the author has mandated for all eternity to appear and rescue the characters caught in the weave of the page—so that they in turn can deliver him from the uproar of his day.

There. The battle is won.

If we wanted to give him the ultimate pleasure, we could fall asleep as he reads to us.

24

"A boy will never be made to understand, of an evening when he is in the midst of a captivating story—a boy will never be made to understand by a demonstration based upon his case alone, that he must interrupt his reading and go to bed."

Kafka noted that in his journal. Little Franz, whose father would have preferred him to spend every night of his life totaling up his accounts.

~ TWO ~

THE NECESSITY OF READING

25

What about our son, upstairs in his room?

He needs to be reconciled with books, too.

The house is quiet, the parents are in bed, the TV is off. He sits alone ... with page 48.

And that damned book report due tomorrow.

Tomorrow ...

He gets out his calculator: 446 minus 48 equals 398.

Three hundred and ninety-eight pages to plow through tonight!

Bravely, he sets about the task. One page chases the next. The words dance between the Walkman's headphones. Their dance is joyless. They have lead shoes on. They collapse one after the other, like horses being shot. Even the drum solo can't get them back on their feet. (Though Dave Grohl is a great drummer!) He pushes on, unconcerned by the bodies of words strewn all around him. The slaughter leaves him unmoved. He slogs his way through the book. Urged on by duty. Page 62, page 63.

He reads.

What is he reading?

The story of Emma Bovary.

The story of a girl who read too much.

She had read Paul et Virginie; *she had dreamed of the bamboo hut, of the negro, Domingo, of Faithful, the dog, but, above all, of the sweet friendship of a dear little brother who would have brought her red-rinded fruit plucked from trees higher than church-towers, or would have run to her barefooted on the sand with a gift of birds' nests.*

The best thing is to phone Terry or Stephanie and ask one of them to lend him her book report tomorrow morning. He could copy it fast before class, no one would know the difference, he's sure they'd do him that favor.

> *When she was thirteen years old, her father had taken her to the city, in order to place her in a convent. They had alighted at an inn in the Saint-Gervais quarter, where at supper they had plates painted with scenes from the life of Mademoiselle de la Vallière. The explanatory legends, broken here and there by the scratches left by many knives, were all designed to glorify religion, sentiment and the splendors of the court.*

The phrase "at supper they had plates painted with scenes" brings a weary smile to his face. Is that all they had to eat—empty plates? They had Mademoiselle Whoosit's life for dinner? He admires his own clever mockery. Considers himself outside his reading. He's wrong. His irony goes right to the heart of the book. They both owe their matching misfortunes to the same source: Emma Bovary saw her plate like a book, and he sees his book like a plate.

26

Meanwhile, back at the ranch ... The scene shifts to the dreaded parent-teacher meeting.

"You see, my son ... my daughter ... when it comes to books ..."

The English teacher understands. Student X doesn't like reading.

"That's why we're so surprised about all this. You see, as a child, he loved reading. He was an absolutely voracious reader, wouldn't you say, dear?"

Dear nods. He was absolutely voracious.

"We've even taken away his television privileges!"

(Television deprivation again. Solving a problem by removing its symptom, not its cause. What a pedagogical gem!)

"That's right. No TV during the school year,

that's one principle we won't give in on."

True, no TV ... but piano lessons from five to six, some nights guitar from six to seven, dance on Wednesday, judo, tennis and soccer on Saturday, a ski trip once the first flakes fall, sailing school as soon as the ice breaks up, art classes on rainy days, educational trips to broaden the mind, work-outs to keep the young body flexible.

But not the palest ghost of a chance for a half-hour alone.

Down with daydreams!

Victory over boredom!

Sweet boredom ...

Long, luxurious boredom ...

That makes all creation possible.

"We make sure he's never bored."

Poor kid!

"We believe ... how can I put it? We believe in giving him an all-around education."

"Useful, dear. I would say a *useful* education."

"Which is why we're here this evening."

"Fortunately, his math grades aren't bad."

"But, of course, when it comes to English ..."

How poor, how sad, how pathetic our effort,

how deep the wound to our pride, as we unwillingly troop off to see the English teacher, with all the pleasure of a chain gang going out to chop weeds in the sun. The teacher listens carefully, nods understandingly, he'd like to cling to his slim sense of self-importance just once in his long and mournful career, if only he could have that glow of self-worth ...

But it is not to be. The fateful words come.

"Do you think a student can pass anyway, even if he fails English?"

27

To each his loneliness. The boy with his contraband notes on his unread book. The parents faced with the shame of his failure. The English teacher with his spurned subject matter.

Where does reading fit in?

28

A young teacher very quickly becomes an old one. Not that the job wears you out faster than any other. The teacher's fatigue comes from hearing so many parents talk about so many children—and, in the process, talk about themselves. It comes from hearing so many life stories, so many divorces, so many family dramas (childhood illnesses, adolescents out of control, adorable daughters whose affection has slipped away), so many failures and proud successes, so many opinions on so many different things. On the necessity of reading in particular, the absolute necessity of reading, on which everyone agrees.

It is the dogma of the age.

Some people never read, and they feel ashamed. Others no longer have the time; now, all they cultivate is regret. Some don't read novels but only useful books: essays, technical manuals, biographies, histories. Some read everything and anything; some read voraciously and it shows; some read only the classics because "there's no better test than the test of time"; some spend their adult years rereading; some read the latest bestseller by Whoosit or Whatsit because, you understand, one has to keep up.

But everyone reads because they know they're supposed to.

It's the dogma.

Including one gentleman who stated that he doesn't read anymore, but only because he'd read so much in the past, and what's the use now that he's finished his studies and found a career, thanks to his own hard work and initiative (as if he'd done it all by himself). But he's still magnanimous enough to recognize that those books, which he no longer needs now, were of great use then. More than useful, indispensable, yes, sir!

"The kid's got to get that into his head!"

The dogma strikes again.

29

As it turns out, the kid does have that embedded in his head. He'd never dream of questioning the dogma, even for a second. At least it looks that way from his essay.

Subject: *Please comment on Flaubert's advice to his friend Louise Collet: "Read if you want to live!"*

The kid agrees with Flaubert, the kid and all his friends agree: *Flaubert was right!* Thirty-five papers with the same opinion: you have to read if you want to live; our ability to read makes us different from the animals; it sets us apart from the savages, the grossly stupid, the hysterically sectarian, those bloody-minded dictators with their galloping materialism. So if you don't want to be like them you'd better read!

To learn.

To do well in school.

To stay informed.

To discover where we came from.

To discover who we are.

To get to know others better.

To discover where we're going.

To maintain the memory of the past.

To understand the present.

To benefit from past experiences.

To keep from repeating our past mistakes.

To save time.

To escape.

To search for the meaning of life.

To understand the foundations of our civilization.

To maintain our thirst for knowledge.

To entertain.

To educate.

To communicate.

To exercise our critical faculties.

The teacher makes approving noises in the margin. *Yes, yes, very good, interesting idea, fair assessment.* And like a child he wants to shout, *More!*

More! Even though this morning he saw the kid in question furiously copying out Stephanie's paper in the hallway; even though his experience has taught him that most of the quotations encountered in the pages of these learned writings come straight from dictionaries invented for just that purpose; even though a quick glance tells him that the examples put forward (*"Use examples taken from your personal reading"*) come from other people's reading; even though his ears are still echoing with the howls of indignation he set off by assigning the novel.

"What? Four hundred pages in two weeks? You're asking the impossible, sir!"

"We've got our math test!"

"And an economics paper to turn in next week!"

Though he knows the role television plays in the adolescent lives of Matthew and Lily, Cedric and Tony and Carmelita, the teacher approves with hearty red ink when Carmelita or Tony or Cedric or Lily or Matthew declares that TV (*"No abbreviations in your papers, please!"*) is the number one enemy of books—and movies, too, when you think about it— because both forms are based on the spectator's amorphous passivity, whereas reading is an act of responsibility (*"Very good!"*).

Here the teacher puts down his pen, looks off into the distance like a daydreaming student and admits—privately, of course—that some films have left him with memories as strong as those from books. How many times has he "reread" *The Deer Hunter, Amarcord, Manhattan, A Room with a View, Babette's Feast* or *Fanny and Alexander*? Their images bear the mystery of signs. He's no expert; he knows nothing of the language of film or the code that movie buffs use. He watched those films with innocent eyes, and his eyes told him quite clearly that here were images whose meanings would never be exhausted; they would touch him anew every time he saw them. The same goes for television images, yes, even TV: the heroism of *Eyes on the Prize,* the Carl Sagan science special, Joe Carter's Series-winning blast off the Wild Thing ...

But time flies. He returns to his grading (who will ever describe the loneliness of the long-distance grader?), but the words begin running together on the page. The arguments are dreadfully repetitive. He grows restless. His students are all reciting the same rosary: *We must read, we must read.* The interminable litany of educational prose. *We must read.* Meanwhile, every sentence proves they've never cracked a book in their lives.

30

"Why work yourself into such a state, dear? Your students are only writing what you tell them to!"

"Which is?"

"That they should read! The dogma! You weren't expecting them to turn out a bunch of papers extolling the virtues of TV, were you?"

"What I want is for them to take off their Walkmans and start reading!"

"That's not what you want. You want them to regurgitate good little book reports on novels you make them read. They have to interpret correctly the poems of *your* choice. And for the final exam, they have to analyze and judiciously summarize novels from *your* list. But who's really encouraging them to read? The final exam? You? Their parents? Of course, nobody's actively discouraging them, but that's not the point. They have to get through the year, that's all. As for the rest, all of you have other fish to fry. Besides, your Gustave Flaubert had other fish to fry, too. Why did he tell poor Louise to go pick up a book? He wanted her out of his hair so he could scribble away at his Bovary, so she wouldn't end up pregnant without his express written consent. That's the truth, and you know it. When Flaubert told Louise to read if she wanted to live, what he really meant was read if you expect *me* to live. Did you explain that to your students? No? Why not?"

She smiles. Puts her hand on his.

"Face the facts, dear. The cult of reading is a product of the oral tradition. You'll have to become its high priest if you want to propagate it."

31

Happily, the very selection of reading matter was such that it did not really make much difference how the schoolmasters handled it: most of the stuff was a deadly bore, anyhow. Almost none of the material we had to study at school was apt to seize or enrich my fancy. Whatever literary background I possess is certainly not due to the sleepy old Wilhelmsgymnasium.

The voices of the great poets fuse in my memory with the voices of those who first transmitted them to me. There are certain masterpieces of the German romantic school which I cannot reread without hearing, once again, the intonations of Mielen's swift and sonorous voice. She was wont to read aloud to us, as long as we were youngsters and it still meant an effort to us to read by ourselves.

. . .

His [my father's] favorites were the Russians. He read to us The Cossacks *by Tolstoy and the strangely primitive, childlike parables of his latest period; we heard stories by Gogol and even one piece by Dostoevsky, the uncanny farce called* A Ridiculous Tale.

No doubt, these eventful evening hours in Father's workroom meant a stimulus, not only to our imaginations but also to our curiosity. Once you have tasted the charm and solace of great literature, you become avid for more stuff of that kind, other ridiculous tales and suggestive parables. So you begin to read by yourself.

So spoke Klaus Mann, son of Thomas, the Magician, and of Mielen, of swift and sonorous voice.

32

Come to think of it, the landscape is pretty depressing. From Rousseau's observations on learning how to read, to Klaus Mann's commentary on the teaching of literature by the Bavarian state, to the barbed comments of the professor's ironic young wife, all the way to the wailing and moaning of today's students, it looks as though school, no matter the age or nation, has had only one role. And that's to teach the mastery of technique and critical commentary and to cut off spontaneous contact with books by discouraging the pleasure of reading. It's written in stone in every land: pleasure has no business in school, and knowledge gained must be the fruit of deliberate suffering.

A defensible position, of course.

No lack of arguments in its favor.

School cannot be a place of pleasure, with all the freedom that would imply. School is a factory, and we need to know which workers are up to snuff. The subjects taught there are knowledge tools. The teachers in charge are the floor bosses, so don't expect them to praise the virtues of free intellectual development when everything, absolutely everything in the school setting—the classes, grades, exams, scales, levels, orientations, streams—enforces the competitive nature of the institution, itself a model of the workaday world.

It does happen that a student meets a teacher whose enthusiasm helps turn mathemetics, for example, into a field of pure study, practically into a branch of the arts. The teacher makes the student love the subject through her own vitality, turning work into pleasure. But this is a chance encounter; it has nothing to do with the spirit of the institution.

It is in the nature of living beings to love life, even in the form of a quadratic equation. But vitality has never been listed on a school curriculum.

Here, function is everything.

Life is elsewhere.

You learn how to read at school.
But what about the love of reading?

33

Read, read, it's your duty to read ...

But what if, instead of demanding that students read, the teacher decided to share the joy of reading?

The joy of reading? Whatever could that mean?

The question demands no small amount of self-knowledge.

Let's begin with a truth that's diametrically opposed to the dogma. When a book changed our lives, we didn't read it *for,* but *against,* something. We read and continue to read as an act of withdrawal, of rejection and defiance. If that makes us fugitives, if reality has little hope of prying us loose from the enchantment of our reading, then so be it, let's be fugitives building a new life, escape artists in search of rebirth.

Every act of reading is an act of resistance. Resistance to what? To the world of random demands.

Social.

Professional.

Psychological.

Sentimental.

Climatic.

Familial.

Domestic.

Fraternal.

Pathological.

Pecuniary.

Ideological.

Cultural.

Or self-conscious.

The act of reading, when well done, preserves us from everything, including ourselves.

Most of all, we read to defeat death.

Kafka read in resistance to his father's mercantile ambitions. Flannery O'Connor read Dostoevsky in resistance to her mother's irony (*"The Idiot*? You would get something called *Idiot*"). Thibaudet read Montaigne in the trenches of Verdun. Henri Mondor

sought solace in Mallarmé during the German occupation and the black market frenzy. A hostage in the
cells of Beirut, Kauffmann the journalist read the
same volume of *War and Peace* over and over again.
Válery tells us of the patient operated on without
anesthesia who "found some comfort or, rather, some
strengthening of his resolve and patience, by reciting
a poem he particularly loved, in the lull between
bouts of unbearable pain." Remember Montesquieu's
confession, co-opted by generations of teachers and
made to serve as the basis for so many dreary disser-
tations: "Study has always been my sovereign remedy
against all disappointments, and I never knew a sor-
row that an hour of reading could not disperse."

More prosaically, a book is a refuge on those
days when rain pelts the windowpane, there is the
quiet enchantment of the pages as the subway car
rocks us, the novel hidden in the drawer of the
secretary's desk, the teacher's stolen moments while
the students work away, and the student in the back
row sneaking a read as she waits to turn in a blank
sheet of paper.

34

Teaching literature is no easy task when reading itself calls for silent retreat.

Reading as an act of communication? More academic nonsense! We conceal what we read, and jealously keep its pleasure to ourselves. Either because it's a private affair, or because, before we can say a word about our experience, we must wait for time to distill its essence. This silence guarantees our privacy. We have finished the book, yet we are still inside it. It is a haven for our secret selves and preserves us from the randomness of the outside world. We read, and enter into silence. We are silent because we've been reading. Who needs those ambush-artists waiting for us to stop so they can ask us, "So? Did you like it? Did you understand it? Now give us a summary!"

At times, our silence is one of humility. Not the
vainglorious humility of professional analysts, but the
private, solitary, sometimes painful knowledge that a
certain book, a certain author, has, as they say,
"changed our lives."

Not to mention this sense of sudden amaze-
ment that leaves us speechless: how can it be that the
book that turned my life upside down didn't move
the rest of the world in a similar way? How can it be
that our century is what it is after Dostoevsky wrote
The Possessed? How can Pol Pot and his kind exist,
now that the character of Peter Verkhovensky is
among us? How could the dreadful gulags have been
built after Chekhov's *Sakhalin Island*? Who dares see
the world in the harsh light of Kafka, where our most
terrible truths flash like sheet metal? Who was listening to Walter Benjamin while horror was loosed upon
the world? After all that, and worse, how is it that the
entire earth hasn't read Robert Antelme's *The
Human Race,* if only to free Carlo Levi's Christ, per-
manently stopped at Eboli?

These books changed our consciousness while
the world went to hell—that in itself is enough to
inspire silence.

So we remain silent.

The only noise is the color commentary of the culture mavens.

You've been at those cocktail parties, the kind where no one has anything to say to anyone else, so they turn books into conversation fodder. A novel is reduced to a seduction strategy! So many silent screams, so much headstrong freedom just so that cock-of-the-walk can cruise that stuck-up babe with a line like, "What do you think of *Journey to the End of the Night?*"

People have died for smaller sins.

35

True, reading is not an immediate act of communication, though it does becomes something we share. But the sharing takes place slowly, over time, and the process is fiercely selective.

If we set aside the great books we read at university, or at the suggestions of the critics, or in response to any other form of advertising, or on the advice of friends, lovers, classmates, even our parents—unless that particular authority was busy shelving away books in the educational closet—this is what we'd see: the books that mean the most to us were usually given by a kindred spirit. And when we're ready to speak, we're more likely to do it with that same person. The nature of feelings, like the desire to read, moves us to preferences. What is love, if not the gift of our preference to those we prefer? Those acts of sharing fill the secret fortress of our freedom. Books and friends inhabit us together.

When a close friend gives us a book, we look for that person between the lines: his tastes, the reason she might have pressed this novel into our hands, the signs of our friendship. Then the story takes over, and we forget the friend who led us into it. That's when the work's strengths take over: we forget how we came to be reading it.

But sometimes, as the years pass, the memory of a book will conjure up the memory of a friend. That's when titles take on human faces.

Let's be honest: the faces aren't always those of a dear friend. Sometimes, rarely, they belong to a critic or professor.

So it was for Pierre Dumayet and his volume *Reading for Everyone,* a book that played an important role in my youth. His eyes and voice and silences communicated the respect he felt for the reader I would soon become, in part thanks to him. That teacher's passion for books gave him patience and us the illusion of love. He must really have liked us students—or at least respected us—if he was willing to give his favorite stories to us!

36

In his biography of the poet Georges Perros, Jean-Marie Gibbal quotes a student from Rennes where Perros taught:

> *He would come in on Tuesday mornings, wind-whipped and frozen stiff on his rusty blue motorcycle. Hunched over in his pea-coat, his pipe in his mouth or in his hand. He would empty a bag of books onto the table. And life would begin.*

Fifteen years later, that student is still under Perros' spell. Smiling as she recalls the memory over a cup of coffee, she travels through time to her own recollections.

"That was how life began: a half-ton of books, pipes, tobacco, a copy of *France-Soir* or *L'Equipe*, keys, notebooks, bills, a sparkplug from his motorcycle ... And out of that mess he drew a book, cast his eyes upon us, gave a laugh that let us know something good was coming, then began to read. He paced as he read, one hand in his pocket, the other one holding the book, outstretched, as if he were literally giving us as a gift. All his reading was a gift. He asked nothing in return. When one of us began to drift off, he stopped reading a second, eyes on the daydreamer, as he whistled a little tune. The object was not to upbraid, but invite the person to return to his world. He never lost sight of us. Even when most absorbed in his reading, he looked at us from over the lines. His voice was deep yet luminous, and slightly hushed. It filled the classroom, as it would have filled an amphitheater, or Notre-Dame cathedral, without him having to pronounce one word louder than the other. Instinctively, he measured the space around him and the space in our minds. He was the natural echo chamber of every book, the incarnation of the text, the book made flesh.

Through his voice, we discovered that every book had been written for us. The discovery was a revelation after the long years of schooling and the literature classes that kept us at a respectful distance from books. What did he do more than our other professors? Nothing. In some ways he did less. The difference was this: he didn't deliver literature with the medicine-dropper of analysis; instead, he filled the glass to the brim. We understood what he read to us. We got *inside* it. There could be no more brilliant explanation of the text than the sound of his voice as he anticipated an author's intention, revealed a hidden meaning, uncovered an allusion. He made misunderstanding impossible. It would have been absolutely unthinkable, after hearing him read Marivaux's *Infidelities,* to mistake the true meaning of the bedroom farce and misinterpret this theater of dissection as light entertainment. The precision of his voice transformed the classroom into a laboratory; the lucidity of his speech urged us to pick up our scalpels and get to work on the living specimen. Not that he added what wasn't there, not that he drew us into the waiting room of Dr. Sade. Still, as we listened to him, we couldn't help seeing the cross-sections of the brains of Arlequin and de Silvia, those Marivaux characters, as if we ourselves were presiding over the vivisection of these two beings.

"We had him an hour a week. That hour was like his backpack: anything could jump out. When he left us at the year's end, I counted up my acquisitions. Shakespeare, Proust, Kafka, Vialatte, Strindberg, Kierkegaard, Molière, Beckett, Marivaux, Paul Valéry, Huysmans, Rilke, Georges Bataille, Julien Gracq, Hardellet, Cervantes, Laclos, Cioran, Chekhov, Henri Thomas, Michel Butor ... I'm remembering as many as I can but I know I've forgotten half of them. In ten years, I haven't heard the tenth of them!

"He talked freely, he read freely, he didn't assume we had a library in our heads. There wasn't a crumb of bad faith in the man. He took us for what we were: young, ignorant students who deserved to know more. There was no talk about cultural heritage or sacred secrets that inhabited the ether. With him, books didn't fall from the sky like manna; he simply picked them up off the ground and offered them to us to read. Everything was present; we were surrounded by the rippling of life. I remember our disappointment at the beginning, when he presented the masters whom our teachers had already told us about: Molière, La Fontaine. But within an hour, they had lost their status as scholastic divinities; they became friends without ever losing their mystery. We simply couldn't live without them. Perros resurrected authors. Arise and go forth. From Apollinaire to Zola, from Brecht to Wilde, they strode into the classroom, very much alive, as if they'd just been at the café across the street. A café where sometimes he'd take us for a second intermission. He didn't play the buddy-buddy professor, that wasn't his type. It was simply his way of teaching what he called his 'course in ignorance.' With him, culture stopped being a state religion, and the bar was a rostrum as proper as any lectern the school had to offer. We listened to him, but we felt no desire to join his order or to put on the clerical collar of knowledge. We just wanted to read. When the class was over, we cleaned out all the bookstores in the county. The more we read, he warned, the more ignorant we would feel, alone on the shore of our ignorance, facing the sea. With him, we weren't afraid to get our feet wet. We dove into books and wasted no time splashing around fearfully in shallow water. I don't know how many of us became teachers. Not many, no doubt, and that's too bad, because he instilled in us the desire to share. To share with the four winds. He couldn't care less about teaching; his ideal was an itinerant university.

"'Why don't we go out for a walk? Let's drop in on Goethe in Weimar, and cuss out God with Kierkegaard's father. Then we can see what the white nights are like on Nevsky Prospect ...'"

37

"Reading, the resurrection of Lazarus, rolling away the stone of words."
— Georges Perros, from *Echancrures*

38

That teacher wasn't just inculcating a body of knowledge; he was giving us what he knew. He was less professor, more master troubadour: one of those word-jugglers who haunted the hostelries on the road to Compostela and sang chronicles of the heroes to illiterate pilgrims.

Since everything has to start somewhere, each year he would gather his little flock at the source of the novel. Like that of the troubadours, his audience *did not yet know how to read.* He opened their eyes. He turned on the lights. He set his students on the road to books, on a pilgrimage without end, a path of encounters.

"He read out loud—that's what made the difference. Right from the start, he trusted our desire to understand ... A teacher who reads out loud lifts you to the level of books. He gives you the gift of reading!"

39

Those of us who read and say we want to spread the love of reading, much of the time we'd rather be commentators, interpreters, analysts, critics, biographers, exegetes of works silenced by our pious respect for their greatness. Imprisoned in the fortress of our expertise, the language of books is replaced by our own language. Instead of letting the intelligence of stories speak through us, we turn to our own intelligence and talk *for* the stories. We have stopped being the messengers of literature, and turned into the fervent guardians of a temple whose miracles we praise with the very words that close its doors. *You must read! You must read!*

40

You must read. To adolescent ears, that is truly begging the question. No matter how brilliant our logic is, it's still begging the question.

The students who have discovered reading through other channels will go on their merry way, enjoying books. The most intellectually curious of them will use the dim light of our explanations to guide their reading.

As for those who don't like to read, the smartest of the bunch will learn how to talk around books, the way we do. They will excel in the inflationary art of commentary (I read ten lines, I grind out ten pages); the reductionist's art of the note (I skim 400 pages, I boil it down to five); the art of judicious quotation (available in freeze-dried form from all better success-merchants). They will learn to wield the scalpel of linear analysis and become experts in navigating from one selected text to the next, a practice that will surely lead to a BA, then an MA, then a doctorate ... but not necessarily to the love of books.

Then there are the other students.

They don't read. The ramifications of the word "meaning" fill them with terror.

They've classified themselves as stupid.

A life without books.

A life without answers.

And soon, a life without questions.

41

Dream this dream with me.

An oral defence for a Ph.D. in modern literature.

The subject of the thesis: "The Registers of Narrative Consciousness in *Madame Bovary.*"

The candidate, a young woman, is sitting at her table, far below the six-member jury, a fossil collection set high above her on their raised platform. To add to the solemnity of the proceedings, let's imagine that the defence takes place in some dusty old amphitheater in some venerable university, like Harvard. An odor of tradition and hallowed oak. The interminable silence of knowledge.

A meager audience of friends and relations is scattered through the theater. Their hearts beat as one with the fearful heart of the young woman. The scene is viewed from above, the woman is below, paralyzed by the terror that she might still possess some shred of ignorance.

Softly, the wood groans. A cough is stifled. An eternity before the ordeal.

The young woman's trembling hand spreads out her notes on the desk. She opens her contribution to knowledge: "The Registers of Narrative Consciousness in *Madame Bovary*."

The chairman of the jury (since it's a dream, let's give him an oxblood toga, the grandeur of years, ermine-trimmed shoulders and a curled wig to set off his craggy face) leans slightly to his right, lifts his colleague's wig and whispers something in his ear. The examiner (a bit younger, in the flush of mature wisdom, with the same toga and wig) nods his head gravely. Then turns and whispers to his neighbor while the chairman murmurs something to the examiner on his left. Consensus is quickly reached at the table.

"The Registers of Narrative Consciousness in *Madame Bovary*." The young woman is too absorbed in her notes, too mortified by the sudden disorder of her thoughts to notice the jury members rising to their feet, climbing down from the platform, approaching then surrounding her. She lifts her head, tries to organize her thoughts; she is caught in the web of their gaze. The fear of not knowing the answers blocks out the strangeness of the situation. Vaguely, she wonders, *What are they doing so close to me?* She immerses herself in her notes again. "The Registers of Narrative Consciousness ..." She has lost the copy of her thesis defence. Such a concise, impenetrable defence! Whatever could she have done with it? Who will restore the clear perspective of her demonstration?

"Miss ..."

The young woman refuses to respond to the chairman. She is searching, searching for the copy of her defence that has blown away in the whirlwind of her knowledge.

"Miss ..."

She seeks. She does not find. "The Registers of Narrative Consciousness in *Madame Bovary* ..." She searches and finds everything else, all her accumulated knowledge. But not the copy of her defence. Her defence cannot be found.

"Miss, please, do listen to me ..."

Is that the chairman's hand on her arm? Since when do chairmen of thesis defence committees put their hands on the arms of young female candidates? And what about that completely unexpected tone of childish pleading in his voice? The examiners begin to fidget in their chairs (for each has carried down a chair, and has come to sit at her side). At last, the young woman looks up.

"Miss, please, forget about the registers of narrative consciousness."

The chairman and his colleagues pull off their wigs. They have the unruly hair of young children, wide eyes, the impatience of starving men.

"Miss, please, tell us the story of Emma Bovary!"

"No, not that! Tell us the story of your favorite novel!"

"Yes, *The Ballad of the Sad Café*! You love Carson McCullers, Miss, tell us the story of the sad café!"

"Then afterwards, you can make us want to read *La Princesse de Clèves* again."

"Make us want to read, Miss."

"Really want to!"

"Tell us the story of *Adolphe*!"

"Read us *Portrait of the Artist,* the chapter about the glasses."

"Kafka! Anything from his diaries."

"Svevo! *Confessions of Zeno*!"

"Read us *Tales from the Zaragossa Manuscript*!"

"Your favorite books!"

"*Ferdydurke*!"

"*A Confederacy of Dunces*!"

"Don't look at the clock, we have all day!"

"Please, please ..."

"Tell us a story!"

"Miss ..."

"Read to us!"

"*The Three Musketeers*!"

"*Panic in Harlem*!"

"*The Book of Laughter and Forgetting*!"

"*Charlie and the Chocolate Factory*!"

"*Alice in Wonderland*!"

"*The House at Pooh Corner*!"

~ THREE ~

THE GIFT OF READING

42

Take a classroom of thirty-five teenagers. Not the kind who've been carefully selected to move effortlessly into the Ivy League, no, the other kind, the ones who've fallen through the cracks at other, better schools, who've gone downstream, who are about to become statistics.

The year begins.

They've ended up here.

In this kind of school.

In front of this teacher.

"Ended up" is the word for it. Thrown overboard when their former classmates set out on the long voyage towards better schools; destination, "Career." Driftwood cast up by the system. Which is how they describe themselves on the forms they fill out the first day.

First name, last name, date of birth.

Past record.

I never was any good in math. Foreign languages don't interest me. I don't have any concentration. I'm no good in writing. There's too much vocabulary in books. (Yes, that complaint again!) *I don't get it about science. I've always flunked spelling. History's okay, except I can't remember dates. I suppose I don't work enough. I never understand the assignments. I messed up a lot of stuff. I like drawing but I don't have the talent. It's too hard for me. I have no memory. I don't have the basics. I don't have any ideas. I don't have any words.*

No future.

That's how they see themselves.

It's over before it begins.

Of course, they're laying it on a little bit thick. That's their style. The personal information sheet, like the diary, calls for self-criticism; it's "in" to be bad. If you put yourself at the bottom of every list, no one will expect anything better from you. At least school has taught them that much: the comfort of fatalism. Nothing suits them better than perpetual failure in math or spelling; saying goodbye to improvement is a small price to pay in order to be spared any effort. And since books contain "too much vocabulary," perhaps they won't be forced to read.

But there's something askew in their self-portrait. These adolescents don't display the low forehead and the heavy jaw that used to fill the fantasies of the *Blackboard Jungle* days.

In their diversity, they're very much creatures of their times. The punks have got their workboots and nose-rings. The upscale crowd is wearing gym shoes that cost a week's salary, some have motorcycle jackets (motorcycle optional), long hair or the spiky look, depending on the week. In pure pre-Raphaelite style, one girl floats inside her father's cotton shirt that reaches all the way down to the torn knees of her Levis. Another girl cultivates the anorexic look ("I am outside this world," her body says), while a third seems to have bought into every cliché in *Vogue* magazine: a dream body and a face to match, both frozen in perfect immobility.

They've barely gotten over chicken pox and mumps, and already they're consuming the latest fashions.

And tall as giants, too! They could use the

teacher's head as a desk! The boys all look like bas-
ketball players, and the girls are already young
women.

Shaking his head, the teacher remembers his
adolescence. It was something vague, frightened,
unsure. He was a paperboy, and his father's shadow
was long ... What did they call his generation, once
it was too late to make noise? The *silent* generation?

These kids seem to think that making noise is
more than a right; it's their obligation.

They can be a little intimidating with their
sheer size and healthy appearance, their slavish
conformity to fashion, their air of maturity. Their hair-
styles, their clothes, their Walkmans, their gadgets,
their private language and self-assurance would
almost convince you that they're better adapted to
their times than the teacher is. That they simply know
more than he does.

About what?

Therein lies the enigma of their young faces.

There's nothing more puzzling than the
appearance of maturity.

If he hadn't been around the block a few times,
the teacher might very well feel out of date with his

silly insistence on verb tenses. But that's the point. He's seen twenty years' worth of children and adolescents, more than three thousand of them. He's seen his share of fashions, seen them fade and return.

One thing never changes: the message on the personal description. The very ostentation of fashion blows their cover. *I'm lazy. I'm stupid. I'm a zero. I've done all I could. Don't waste your time. My past has no future* ...

They don't love themselves. And they proclaim it with childish persistence.

They're between two worlds. Having lost contact with both. They're cool, no doubt about it, way cool. School messes up their minds, its demands bust their balls. They're not kids anymore, but they slave away, forever waiting to grow up.

They'd like to be free; they feel abandoned instead.

43

Of course, they don't like to read. Too much vocabulary in books. Too many pages, too. Too many books, when it comes down to it.

No, definitely, they don't like to read.

That's what the raised hands suggest when the teacher asks, "Who here doesn't like to read?"

Nearly all the hands go up. That's a challenge in itself. A few aren't raised (the Anorexic's, among others), but that's out of sheer indifference to the question.

"In that case," says the teacher, "since you don't like to read, I'll read you the books myself."

With no further ado, he opens his bag and takes out an enormous book, a regular doorstop, a brick with a glossy cover. The most bookish-looking book you could imagine.

"Are you ready?"

They don't believe their eyes or their ears. Is he going to read them *all* that? It'll take him all year! They're confused. The atmosphere is tense. There's no such thing as a teacher who spends the whole year reading. Either he's lazier than they are, or he's got something up his sleeve. This is some kind of trap. There's got to be a daily vocabulary list and a comprehension test at the end.

The students glance at each other. A few of them, just in case, take out a sheet of paper and prepare their ballpoints.

"Don't bother taking notes. Just try to listen, that's all."

Now comes the problem of *attitude*. What do you do with your body in a classroom without the props of a ballpoint pen and a sheet of lined paper? What do you do with yourself under such circumstances?

"Sit back, make yourself comfortable, relax."

Relax? That's a good one!

Curiosity gains the upper hand. The Punks ask, "You're going to read us that whole book … *out loud?*"

"I don't see how you could hear me if I read it to myself."

Discreet laughter. The Anorexic doesn't go for that bait. In a stage whisper heard by everyone, she declares, "We're too old for that kind of stuff."

That's the usual prejudice among those who have never been given the gift of reading. The rest of us know you're never too old for that pleasure.

"If, in ten minutes, you still think you're too old, raise your hand, and we'll go on to something else, okay?"

"What kind of book is it?" Reebok asks, as if he'd read them all.

"A novel."

"What's it about?"

"It's hard to say if you haven't read it. All right, are you ready? That's enough talk. Let's hit it."

They're skeptical, but willing to try.

"*In eighteenth-century France there lived a man who was one of the most gifted and abominable personalities in an era that knew no lack of gifted and abominable personages . . .*"

44

... In the period of which we speak, there reigned in the cities a stench barely conceivable to us modern men and women. The streets stank of manure, the courtyards of urine, the stairwells stank of moldering wood and rat droppings, the kitchens of spoiled cabbage and mutton fat; the unaired parlors stank of stale dust, the bedrooms of greasy sheets, damp featherbeds, and the pungently sweet aroma of chamberpots. The stench of sulphur rose from the chimneys, the stench of caustic lyes from the tanneries, and from the slaughterhouses came the stench of congealed blood. People stank of sweat and unwashed clothes; from their mouths came the stench of rotting teeth, from their bellies that of onions, and from their bodies, if they were no longer

very young, came the stench of rancid cheese and sour milk and tumorous disease. The rivers stank, the marketplaces stank, the churches stank, it stank beneath the bridges and in the palaces. The peasant stank as did the priest, the apprentice as did his master's wife, the whole of the aristocracy stank, even the king himself stank, stank like a rank lion, and the queen like an old goat, summer and winter ...

45

Dear Mr. Süskind, thank you so much! From your pages emanates a perfume that tickles both the nose and the funny-bone. Never did your *Perfume* have more enthusiastic readers than those thirty-five teenagers who never would have read you. After the first ten minutes, I think you should know, the Anorexic decided you were just perfect for her age group. It was touching, watching her twist her mouth this way and that, so that her laughter would not drown out the sound of your prose. Reeboks opened his eyes and his ears, and when one of his pals laughed a little too loud, he warned him to shut his trap. Round about page 25, when you're comparing your Jean-Baptiste Grenouille, who's then boarding at Madame Gaillard's rooming-house, to a tick lying in constant ambush (you remember, "The lonely tick, which, wrapped up in itself, huddles in its tree, blind, deaf, and dumb, and simply sniffs, sniffs all year long, for miles around, for the blood of some passing animal ..."), right at that part, when we first descend into the dank recesses of Jean-Baptiste Grenouille's mind, the Punks fell asleep, their heads on their folded arms. Perfectly relaxed, their breathing deep and regular. No, no, don't wake them up, there's nothing better than a good sleep after a lullaby. That's one of the great pleasures of being read to. The Punks returned to the trusting age of childhood again ... and they woke up as children, too, when the bell rang the end of the hour.

"Oh, hell, I fell asleep! What happened at the Gaillard woman's place?"

46

And my thanks to all of you, Márquez, Calvino, Stevenson, Dostoevsky, Saki, Amado, Gary, Fante, Dahl, Roché, the dead and the quick, gratitude to all of you! Of the thirty-five non-readers, not a single one waited for the teacher to get to the end of one of your books; they all finished every book themselves. Why put off a pleasure till next week when you can have it tonight?

"Who's this Süskind guy?"

"Is he alive?"

"What else did he write?"

"What kind of name is Süskind? Is he English? It sounded like English to me!"

(And thank you, translators, speakers in tongues, you who let us travel!)

The semester passes ...

"*Chronicle of a Death Foretold*—it's great! How about *One Hundred Years of Solitude*—what's that all about?"

"I love that Fante guy. *West of Rome* really cracked me up!"

"Romain Gary, *Madame Rosa,* great stuff."

"Roald Dahl is too much. The story about the woman who kills her man with the frozen leg of lamb, then serves the murder weapon to the cops for dinner—what an idea!"

Of course, of course, their critical faculties are not yet honed, but that'll come, just let them read, the rest will fall into place.

"Really, when it comes down to it, *The Cloven Viscount,* and *Dr. Jekyll and Mr. Hyde,* and *The Picture of Dorian Gray,* they're really about the same things. Good and evil, and double identity, and your conscience and temptation, social morality, all that stuff, isn't that true?"

"It is."

"What about Raskolnikov? Wouldn't you say he's a romantic character?"

See. It's all falling into place.

47

There was no miracle. The teacher doesn't deserve much in the way of praise. The pleasure of reading was close at hand, held hostage in those adolescent attics by a secret and very old fear: the fear of not understanding.

They had forgotten what a book was, and what it had to offer. They had forgotten that, above all else, a novel *tells a story.* They didn't realize that a novel must be read as a novel, and that its first job is to quench our thirst for stories.

To fulfill that need, they turned to the small screen. It did its assembly-line job, grinding out cartoons, series, soap operas and thrillers in a string of interchangeable stereotypes. That was their ration of fiction. It filled their heads the way fast food fills the stomach. It stuffed them, but it didn't stick to the ribs. Digestion was immediate. But they were hungry again right after the meal.

With the public reading of *Perfume,* Süskind seemed to be standing there before them. He was a story, a wonderful tale, comic and baroque, but most of all a *voice,* Süskind's voice (later, in their term papers, they'll call that a "style"). A story, yes—but a story told by someone.

"The beginning's incredible: 'the bedrooms stank, the people stank, the rivers stank, the market-places stank, the churches stank, the king stank ...' And they always tell us to avoid repetition! But it's great anyway, isn't it? I mean, it's funny, but it's still great."

True, the charm of style adds to the pleasure of the story. After the last page, the echo of that voice remains with us. And Süskind's voice, even through the double filter of the translation and the teacher's voice, is not the same as Márquez's voice—"You can tell right away!"—or Calvino's. That's how they feel it. Stereotypes all speak the same language, but Süskind, Márquez and Calvino speak their own language, and they speak to me alone, tell their story just for me, the Anorexic, the Preppie, the Biker without a bike or the Punk. I can distinguish their voices and decide which among them I prefer.

> *Many years later, as he faced the firing squad, Colonel Aureliano Buendía was to remember that distant afternoon when his father took him to discover ice. At that time Macondo was a village of twenty adobe houses, built on the bank of a river of clear water that ran along a bed of polished stones, which were white and enormous, like prehistoric eggs.*

"I know that first sentence of *One Hundred Years of Solitude* by heart! With those stones, 'like prehistoric eggs.'"

Thank you, Señor Márquez, for starting the game that will last all year long. Read, remember and recite the first sentences or favorite paragraphs of one of your best-loved novels.

"For me, it's the beginning of *Adolphe,* you know, the part about being shy. 'I did not know that my father was timid, even with his son, and that often, having waited a long while for some sign of affection from me which his apparent coldness seemed to prohibit, he would leave me, his eyes moist with tears, and complain to others that I did not love him.' That's exactly like my father and me!"

Once we stood before a closed book, our eyes shut. Now we are free to wander among the pages.

The teacher's voice helped with the reconciliation. It spared them the effort of figuring out the words, it sketched out the situations, described the setting, took on the characters' voices, pointed out the themes, accentuated the nuances, acted the way developing fluid acts when the blank paper is in the pan.

But soon the teacher's voice begins to create interference. A kind of static that gets in the way of more subtle kinds of pleasure.

"It helps when you read to us. But I'm just as happy to be alone with the book, afterwards."

The teacher's voice—the gift of the story—reconciled them with writing. It made them want to use their secret, silent alchemist's voices again, the same ones that, ten years earlier, were amazed that *mommy* written on a sheet of paper could be their mother in real life.

The pleasure of the novel resides in this paradoxical intimacy. The author and I. Words are alone, and they need my silent, solitary voice to tell their story.

The teacher is just a go-between. Now it's time for him to steal away on his tiptoes.

48

We conquered the fear of not understanding. One more phobia remains before the students can be reconciled with private reading: the fear of length.

The time it takes to read. The book seen as an eternity.

When they saw the teacher pull *Perfume* out of his bag, they thought an iceberg had come into the room. Mind you, he'd chosen the largest, most luxurious hardcover edition, with the widest margins and the biggest type, a mountain in the eyes of those non-readers, promising endless hours of punishing effort.

But when he started reading it, the iceberg seemed to melt away in his very hands.

Time is no longer time. Minutes rush by in seconds. Forty pages are read, and the hour's already gone.

The teacher's doing 40 an hour.

Which makes 400 pages in ten hours. At five hours a week, he could read 3,000 pages in the fall term. Or 7,000 during the school year! Seven novels at 1,000 pages each! In only five hours of weekly reading!

An amazing discovery. It changes everything. When you break it down, it doesn't take long to read a book. If I read one hour a day, in a week I'll have finished a 280-page novel. I can read the same book in only three days if I put in a little over two hours a day. That would make 560 pages in six working days. And if the book happens to be extra cool—"*The Sound and the Fury,* sir, now that's a real cool book!"—and I take off four hours on a Sunday to read (which is possible, since the suburbs where the Punks live are dead on Sundays, and the Preppie's parents drag him off to the country to bore him to death), that adds another 160 pages, for a grand total of 720!

Or 540, if I do 30 per hour, a reasonable speed.

Or 360 if I cruise at 20 per hour.

"I can do 360 pages a week. What about you?"

Count the pages, kids, count them all ... novelists do the same thing. You should see them when they hit page 100. Page 100 is the Cape Horn of novel-writing! They uncork an imaginary bottle, dance a discreet jig, snort and sniffle like a drafthorse then get back to it, they dive into their inkwells for page 101. (A drafthorse diving into an inkwell is an astonishing image, admit it!)

Count the pages, yes ... At first they're amazed at how many they've covered. Later, they'll be dismayed by how few are left. Only 50 pages left! You'll see for yourself. There's nothing more rewarding than that sadness: *War and Peace,* two fat volumes, and only 50 pages left to read.

They read slower and slower, but it's too late.

Natasha ends up marrying Pierre Bezuhov, and the final curtain falls.

49

That's all very well, but where in my busy day will I find time for my hour of reading? Where should I steal it from? My friends? TV? Traveling? Family evenings? Homework?

Where will I find the time to read?

It's a serious problem.

Serious, but false.

If you have to ask yourself where you'll find the time, it means the desire isn't there. Because, if you look at it more carefully, no one has the time to read. Children don't, teenagers don't, adults don't. Life is a perpetual plot to keep us from reading.

"Reading. I'd love to, but what with my job, the kids, the housework, I don't have the time."

"You have so much time to read—I envy you!"

How is it that Ms X, who works, runs errands, raises kids, drives her car, loves three men, goes to her dentist appointment, is moving next week—how is it that she finds time to read, while this chaste, retired, coupon-clipping bachelor doesn't?

Time spent reading is always time stolen. Like time spent writing, or loving, for that matter.

Stolen from what?

From life's obligations.

Which is probably why the subway—the very symbol of life's many obligations—is the world's largest reading room.

Time spent reading, like time spent loving, increases our lifetime.

If we were to consider love from the point of view of our schedule, who would bother? Who among us has time to fall in love? Yet have you ever seen someone in love not take the time to love?

I've never had the time to read. But no one has ever kept me from finishing a novel I loved.

Reading does not belong to the societal organization of time. Like love, it is a way of being.

The issue is not whether or not I have the time to read (after all, no one will ever give me that time), but whether I will allow myself the joy of being a reader.

The spiky-haired Punk in workboots put a quick and decisive end to that circular conversation.

"Time to read? It's in the bag!"

And he pulled his latest acquisition (Jim Harrison's *Legends of the Fall* in a paperback edition) from his backpack.

The Biker without a bike nodded approvingly.

"When you buy a jacket, you've got to make sure the pockets are the right size."

50

According to current slang, a book is a *brick*. A *doorstop*.

But in the right hands, it can be as light as a cloud.

51

We have to satisfy one condition for this reconciliation to take place: we must ask for nothing in return. Absolutely nothing. Erect no wall of prior knowledge around books. Ask not a single question. Do not assign the smallest scrap of homework. Do not add a single word to the pages that have been read. No value judgments, no vocabulary explanations, no textual analysis, no biographical notes. It is strictly forbidden to talk around the book.

Reading is a gift.

Read, and wait.

Curiosity can't be forced. It must be awakened.

Read, and trust the eyes that open slowly, the faces that light up, the questions that will begin to form and give way to other questions.

If the pedagogue in us has a hard time not "presenting the work in its total context," persuade that little voice that the only context that counts, right now, is this moment in this classroom.

The pathways to knowledge do not end in this classroom; they should start from it.

For the time being, I am reading novels to an audience that thinks it doesn't like reading. Nothing important can be taught until I've defeated that illusion and completed my work as a go-between.

Once these teenagers are reconciled with books, they'll gladly take the road that leads from the novel to its author, from the author to his or her era, from the story they've read to the many meanings it contains.

Be prepared.

And get ready for an avalanche of questions.

"Was this Stevenson British?"

"He came from Scotland."

"What century?"

"The nineteenth. Victorian times."

"I heard Victoria was queen forever ..."

"For sixty-four years, from 1837 to 1901."

"Sixty-four years!"

"She'd been queen for thirteen years when Stevenson was born, and he died seven years before she did. You're fifteen now. If she ascended to the throne today, you'd be seventy-nine at the end of her reign. That was at a time when people didn't live as long as they do now. And she wasn't the jolliest of queens either."

"That's why Hyde was born from a nightmare!"

The Anorexic had spoken. The Preppie was amazed.

"How did you know that?"

"We have ways of finding things out," the Anorexic said enigmatically.

And then, with a discreet smile, she added, "I happen to know it was one hell of a nightmare. When Stevenson woke up, he locked himself in his office and wrote the first version of the book in exactly two days. His wife made him throw it in the fireplace because he made Hyde into someone who was just too cool, pillaging and raping and slashing everything he came across. That old queen wouldn't have gone for that. That's why he had to invent Jekyll."

52

Reading out loud isn't enough. You have to actually tell stories, offer your treasures, spread them out before an unknowing public. Hear ye, hear ye, come and admire, a real story!

There's no better way of stimulating a reader's appetite than holding out the promise of an orgy of reading.

Of Georges Perros, his grateful former student said this: "He went much further than simply reading. He actually told the story. He related *Don Quixote* to us. *Madame Bovary,* too. They were great masses of critical intelligence, but when he related them, they sounded like regular stories. He turned Sancho Panza into a wineskin of life, and the Knight of Sad Countenance into a bony stick armed with the most painful self-assurance. He told Emma Bovary's story in a way that made her more than just a silly goose romanced by the dust of old reading rooms; she became a complex of burning energy. In Perros' voice, we heard Flaubert cackling over this enormous mess of a human being."

Dear librarians, guardians of the temple, I'm glad that all the titles in the world have found their pigeon-holes in the perfect organization of your collective memory (for how would I find my way without you, I who have Jell-O for a memory?). It is wondrous indeed that you know where to find all the themes you've carefully arranged on the shelves around you. But it would be good, for once, to hear you tell the story of your favorite novels to the visitors who've lost their way in the forest of potential reading. Just as it would be good if you'd regale them with the memories of your favorite books. Be tellers of tales, be magicians, and the books will jump off your shelves into the readers' waiting hands.

Telling a novel's story is simple. Sometimes three little words can do the trick.

Memories of childhood and summer. The calm afternoon hours. My older brother lying on his stomach on the bed, chin resting on his hands, absorbed in a fat paperback. His little brother, a gadfly, asks, "What are you reading?"

"*The Rains Came.*"

"Any good?"

"It's great!"

"What's it about?"

"Some guy. At the beginning he drinks a lot of whisky, then at the end he switches to water."

That's all I needed to know. I spent the rest of that summer soaked to the skin by Louis Bromfield's *The Rains Came.* I stole it from my big brother, and he hasn't seen it since.

53

That's all well and good, Süskind, Stevenson, Márquez, Dostoevsky, Fante, Chester Himes, Selma Lagerlöf, Italo Calvino, all those novels read pell-mell, without the benefit of study; all those stories told, an anarchist's feast of reading for the sheer pleasure of it. But where's the method, for goodness sake, where's the *method?* The weeks streak by and the syllabus of required reading hasn't even been scratched. The terror of wasting time, the fear of a syllabus unsatisfied.

Don't panic. The syllabus will be covered, the required books will be read.

Despite what the Punks and Preppies thought, the teacher is not going to spend the whole year reading. Too bad! Why did the pleasure of solitary, silent reading have to intrude so quickly? No sooner had the teacher begun reading out loud than the students rushed off to the bookstore to buy "the end" before the next class. No sooner had he told a story or two—"Whatever you do, don't reveal the end!"— than the students devoured the books that the stories came from.

The teacher shouldn't be deceived by this sudden enthusiasm. He's no magician; he hasn't transformed one hundred percent of his non-readers into book-lovers. At the beginning, everyone read. They overcame their fears; they read from a sense of enthusiasm and emulation. Like it or not, they probably read to get on the teacher's good side. The wise instructor won't rest on his laurels. Nothing cools faster than adolescent infatuation; he's seen that happen more than once. But for now, everyone is reading enthusiastically under the influence of that particular magic that turns a class into a self-confident, reading being, a single healthy individual, without losing the thirty distinct individualities contained therein. Which does not mean they will all grow into adults who like to read. Other pleasures may take over from the pleasure of reading. But for these first few weeks of the school year, the act of reading—remember that phrase?—no longer terrorizes the students. They are reading, and some of them are doing it quite quickly.

What's with these novels that makes them candidates for quick reading? Are they easy to read? What does that mean? Is *The Story of Gösta Berling* easy to read? Is *Crime and Punishment* easy to read? Easier than *The Stranger* or *The Red and the Black*? Not at all. First, they have this virtue: they're not on the syllabus. A major virtue for the Anorexic and her friends who quickly classify any work chosen by the academic authorities to expand their culture as "a pain in the butt." Poor syllabus. It's not its fault. How could Rabelais or Dickens or Camus be pains in the butt? Fear is what makes them that way. Fear of not understanding, fear of the wrong answer, fear of the reading police, fear of English as a heavy, opaque subject. Fear smears the sentences of the books and drowns the meaning in the details.

The Preppie and the Biker were astonished when the teacher told them that *The Stranger,* which they'd just devoured with delight, was the bane of their fellow-students' existence in France, simply because it's on their syllabus. Imagine this: a Preppie or a Biker in Paris sneaking a read of *The Scarlet Letter,* while his teacher vainly pounds away about the virtues of Camus!

As they move through the world of free reading, travelers without passports crossing into foreign works (Russian, French, Italian and Spanish books have the advantage of being farther from the dreaded syllabus), the students, reconciled with reading, circle ever closer to the works that must be read for the school program. Soon they will dive into Hawthorne or Melville without a second thought, for the simple reason that their books have become novels like all the others, as good as any other. (Or maybe even better, for the stigmata of adultery is sure to bring a shiver of forbidden delight in this world where everything is permitted, even expected.)

> *Dear Mr. Hawthorne,*
>
> *In case you haven't heard the news, I'd like to tell you about a certain high school class of Walkman-loving non-readers who put your* Scarlet Letter *in the top ten, some time after you originally wrote it.*

The required texts will be covered. The techniques of essay writing and textual analysis (those lovely, crisscross grids of literary meaning), interpretive commentary and abstract discussion will be duly transmitted. The whole mechanism will be well oiled. So when the fateful day of the final exam comes, and the proper performance is demanded, the students will have their chance to show that they not only read for pleasure, but that they understood, and best of all, they made the *effort* to understand.

The issue of what they understood (the proof of the pudding) is an interesting one. Understood the book? Yes, of course. But once they were reconciled with reading, and books lost their fearful status as insoluble riddles, they began to see that the effort to capture meaning can be a pleasure. When they conquered the fear of not understanding, effort and pleasure became powerful allies. My effort increases my pleasure, and the pleasure of understanding makes me drunk with the burning solitude of my effort.

They've understood something else, too. They've acquired the sly knowledge of how the system works, the art and method of talking around a book and bumping up their value on the examination market. Why hide it? That's one of the goals of the exercise. When it comes to final exams and job interviews, to understand means to know what is expected of us. When a text has been understood, it means we've intelligently negotiated it. The student looks for a pay-off as she bargains with the examiner, slipping him a sidelong glance after serving up an intelligent interpretation—not showily intelligent, mind you— of a passage with a particularly opaque reputation. ("He looks happy, let's ride this train, I'm on my way to an A.")

The teaching of literature in schools is as much strategy as it is the intelligent reading of a text. More often than not, a "bad" student is one with a woeful lack of tactical skills. In a panic, unable to provide what the system demands of him, he mixes up learning and culture. Pushed aside by the school system, he soon sees himself as an untouchable in the world of reading. He concludes that books belong to the elite and chooses a life without them because, once, he could not discuss them when exam time came.

54

What's more, books aren't written so that our sons and daughters can compose essays on them. Books are there to be read, should readers be so inclined.

Our knowledge, schooling, social life and career are one thing. Our private reading and culture are another. It's great to grind out BAs, MAs and PhDs, society needs those people. But it's much better to open the pages of books to new readers.

Through their long years of education, grade-school and high-school students are made to produce more than enough analysis and commentary to frighten them away from books. Our century certainly hasn't helped things. It's made theory lord and master, to the point where we've lost sight of what we're actually theorizing about. This maddening buzz carries the misleading name of *communication.*

To talk to teenagers about books and ask them to respond can be very useful, but it is not an end in itself. The end is the work. The book they hold in their hands. And the most important of their rights, when it comes to reading, is the right to remain silent.

ss

At the start of the school year, I often ask my students to describe a bookshelf. More often than not, they describe a wall. A wall of knowledge, painstakingly built, absolutely impenetrable, a cliff that would repel any invader.

"What about a reader? Describe a reader to me."

"A real reader?"

"If you like, but I don't know what you mean by a real reader."

The most deferential students describe the Lord God himself, an antediluvian hermit sitting for all eternity on a mountain of books whose meaning he's sucked dry, and who has the answer to every question. Others, less reverent, portray someone suffering from an autism so deep that he crashes into the walls of everyday life. Still others sketch a portrait of all the things a reader is not: not athletic, not alive, not fun; someone who doesn't care about food or clothes or cars, TV or music or friends. Some are more tactical in their approach: to impress their teacher, they construct an ideal image of the Reader with his increased awareness and well honed mind, both of which he has acquired thanks to books. Some students combine the images. But not one, not a single one, describes himself or herself, or a member of her family, or any of those readers he sees every day on the subway.

When I ask them to describe a book, it's as if a UFO had landed in the classroom. A mysterious object, deceptively simple, an intruder both powerful and dangerous, a sacred artifact, demanding exaggerated care and respect, to be placed with reverence on the shelves of an immaculate library, and there to be worshipped by a sect devoted to cultivating the enigmatic.

The Holy Grail.

What do you expect?

It's our job to bring their vision of books back down to earth and show them how we book-lovers really treat them.

56

Few objects inspire a feeling of absolute ownership the way books do. Once we get our hands on them, books become our slaves. Slaves, yes, for they are alive, yet no one would dream of freeing them, for their flesh is fashioned from dead trees. As objects of our outlandish love and fury, they suffer terrible abuse. How do I abuse thee? Let me count the ways. I dog-ear your pages (I know it's a sin, but that way I never lose my place). I put my coffee cup on your cover and leave little halos there. I smear breakfast jam and leave streaks of sun-tan oil on you. There is a track of telltale fingerprints on each of your pages, and tobacco-stains from the pipe I was smoking. And what about the luxury edition sadly drying on the radiator, which you accidentally dropped into the bathtub? (Yes, dear, *your* bath, but *my* copy of Swift.) Its margins busy with scribbled notes, now fortunately illegible, its paragraphs highlighted by fluorescent markers. And what of this poor volume, crippled for life, having spent a week face-down with its spine in an unnatural position? And its companion, its once-luminous cover now shrouded in a ghastly plastic sheet with an oily sheen? On the bed, a pile of books is heaped like fallen sparrows. A stack of old paperbacks is being eaten alive by mildew in my basement. Forlorn childhood treasures that no one reads anymore have been exiled to a cottage where no one ever goes. And all those others in the second-hand shops, slaves auctioned over and over again ...

We put our own books through everything. But when other people mistreat theirs—that's intolerable!

Not long ago, I witnessed a woman throwing an enormous novel out the window of a speeding car. She had spent so much money on the word of trustworthy critics—only to be cruelly disappointed. The father of novelist Tonino Benacquista went so far as to smoke Plato. A prisoner of war somewhere in Albania, he had a few shreds of tobacco in his pocket, a copy of the *Cratylus* (what it was doing there, God only knows!), a match and *voilà:* a new way of dialoguing with Socrates using smoke signals.

Another tragedy of that same war, worse still. Alberto Moravia and Elsa Morante, forced to hide for several months in a shepherd's hut, were able to save just two books: the Bible and *The Brothers Karamazov.* This gave rise to a terrible dilemma. Which of these two monuments would they use as toilet paper? Cruel or not, a choice had to be made. With heavy hearts, they made it.

However sacred the halo surrounding books, who could stop Pepe Carvalho, the beloved creation of the Spaniard Manuel Vasquez Montalban, from lighting a cheery fire every evening with the pages of his favorite works?

Such is the price of love, the wages of sharing.

Once a book falls into our possession, it is ours, the same way children lay their claim: "That's *my* book." As if it were organically part of them. That must be why we have so much trouble returning borrowed books. It's not exactly theft (of course not, we're not thieves, what are you implying?); it's simply a slippage in ownership or, better still, a transfer of substance. That which belonged to someone else becomes mine when I look at it. And if I like what I read, naturally I'll have difficulty giving it back.

That's the way we civilians treat our books. Publishers do no better. They guillotine the paper at the edge of the text so their mass-market lines will be more profitable, producing marginless books whose type gasps for breath. They bulk up their tiny novels to make readers believe they're getting their money's worth (a text drowning in white space, the sentences wandering in the desert). They add gaudy, embossed, die-cut covers that can be spotted half a block away, that cry out, "Pick me up! Take me home!" They manufacture book-club editions with spongy paper and thick cardboard covers dressed up with inane illustrations. They turn out "limited" editions by decorating fake-leather bindings with an orgy of gold-stamped curlicues.

As a product of our hyperactive consumer society, books are treated about as well as a hormone-injected chicken, and are certainly respected less than a nuclear missile. The hormone-fed chicken that reaches maturity in a day is a perfect comparison when you think of those thousands of instant books that come out a week after the queen kicked the bucket or the president got the heave-ho.

The book is a commercial object, just as ephemeral as any other consumer item. Sent off to be pulped if it doesn't "take off" within a week, it usually dies without having been read.

As for the way academia treats books, why not ask a writer what she thinks? Here's what Flannery O'Connor wrote the day she discovered that students were being assigned her work:

> *If teachers are in the habit of approaching a story as if it were a research problem for which any answer is believable so long as it is not obvious, then I think students will never learn to enjoy fiction.*

57

So much for books.

Let's talk about readers.

We've described how we treat books; now let's consider how we read them.

When it comes to reading, we grant ourselves every right in the book, including those we withhold from the young people we claim to be teaching.

1. The right to not read.
2. The right to skip pages.
3. The right to not finish a book.
4. The right to reread.
5. The right to read anything.
6. The right to escapism.
7. The right to read anywhere.
8. The right to browse.

9. The right to read out loud.

10. The right to not defend your tastes.

I'll stop at ten. A nice round figure, that also happens to be the sacred number of the famous Commandments. Except that this is a list of things you *can* do.

If we want our sons, our daughters, all young people to read, we must grant them the same rights we grant ourselves.

~ FOUR ~

THE READER'S BILL OF RIGHTS

I.

The Right to Not Read

Any self-respecting list must begin with the right *not* to exercise what is being offered—in this case, the right to read. Without this option, we wouldn't have a bill of rights but an insidious trap.

In any case, most readers invoke the right to not read on a daily basis. No matter how essential we writers think we are, in a competition between a good book and a mediocre soap opera, the latter will come out on top more often than we'd care to admit. Besides, who can read all the time? Our periods of reading often alternate with times when the mere sight of a book conjures up indigestion and exhaustion.

But the real point is elsewhere.

We all know people who, despite being respectable, well educated, even eminent, some of them owners of magnificent libraries, either don't read or read so little that we'd never dream of giving them a book as a gift. Such people simply don't read. Perhaps because they don't feel the need to, or because they are too busy with things that overwhelm or obsess them, or because they have another passion and want to remain faithful to it. Whatever the reason, they don't like to read. That doesn't mean we should spurn them; that doesn't mean they can't offer their share of delights. (They do have certain advantages. They're not always asking us about the book we happen to be reading, and they spare us their ironic comments about our favorite novelist. And they don't consider us half-wits because we didn't rush out and snap up the latest book by Whatchamacallit, just published by Black Hole Press, lavishly praised by the post-structuralist critic, Abraham Whitepage.) Such people are just as human as we are. They care about the world's suffering; they support the rights of the individual and respect them in their daily lives. That in itself is no mean feat. There's only one problem: they don't read. But that's their business.

The idea that reading humanizes a person is a good one, even if there are some depressing exceptions to that rule. In general, we're all a little more human, we all have a bit more solidarity with our species (we're less "beastly," if you like) after we've read Chekhov.

But that doesn't mean the opposite is true: that any individual who doesn't read should automatically be considered a monster or a cretin. If so, we'd be transforming reading into a moral obligation, and that's the top of the slippery slope that leads to judging the morality of books themselves according to criteria that have no respect for another inalienable right: the right to create. Then we'd be the monsters—reading monsters, but monsters all the same. And God knows there's no shortage of that kind in our world.

In other words, *the freedom to write cannot coexist with the obligation to read.*

The duty of education is to teach children how to read, to introduce them to literature and to give them the means to judge freely whether or not they feel the need for books. Though we can recognize that someone might reject the world of books, no one must feel that that world is rejecting him.

To be excluded from books—including those we might not want to read—is terribly sad; it is lonely alienation from the fertile solitude of reading.

2.

The Right to Skip Pages

I read *War and Peace* for the first time when I was twelve or thirteen years old, probably thirteen. From the beginning of summer vacation, I had watched my older brother (the one I stole *The Rains Came* from) slowly disappear into that enormous novel. His gaze became as distant as that of an explorer who has long since lost the desire to see his homeland again.

"Is it really that good?"

"It's great!"

"What's it about?"

"Some girl who loves one guy but marries another."

My brother always did have the knack for quick

summaries. If publishers were to hire him to write their blurbs, those pathetic advertising devices on the back covers of books, it would save us all a lot of useless blather.

"You want to lend it to me?"

"It's yours."

I was at boarding school, so that was a most valuable present. Two thick volumes that would keep me warm all through the year. Five years older than I am, my brother was no fool (he still isn't), and he knew very well that *War and Peace* could not be boiled down to a love story, no matter how well crafted it was. But he knew I loved the swell of grand sentiment, and that his cryptic formulation would arouse my curiosity. (A true teacher, in my sense of the word.) I'm sure it was the calculated mystery of his summary that made me temporarily put aside my boyhood classics and adventure books to jump head-first into the novel. "A girl who loves one guy but marries another"—who could resist? I wasn't disappointed, though my brother had gotten his figures wrong. In fact, four of us loved Natasha: Prince Andrey, the despicable Anatole (but could you call his feelings love?), Pierre Bezuhov and me. Since I had

no chance of coming out on top, I was forced to iden-
tify with the other three (except for Anatole, who was
a real bum!).

The experience was made sweeter by the
stolen hours, reading by flashlight under the covers
draped like a tent in the middle of a dormitory with
fifty other dreamers, snorers and fidgeters. The mon-
itor's outpost where a nightlight drowsed lay close
by, but so what? In love, it's all or nothing. I can still
feel the weight and thickness of those volumes. I
had the paperback version, with Audrey Hepburn's
pretty face watched over covetously by a princely Mel
Ferrer with his heavy, predatory, lover's eyelids. I
skipped three-quarters of the book. Natasha's heart
alone interested me. I mourned for Anatole a little
when they cut off his leg. I damned that hard-headed
Prince Andrey when he stood up straight as the
cannonball came whistling in at the battle of
Borodino. ("Hit the dirt, for Christ's sake, it's going to
blow, you can't do that to her, she loves you!") I was
interested in love and war; I skipped over politics and
strategy. Clausewitz's theories shot high over my
head. But I avidly followed Pierre Bezuhov's marital
misfortunes with his wife Hélène (Hélène wasn't very

cool, I thought, she wasn't very cool at all). And let Tolstoy rattle on alone about Mother Russia's agrarian problems.

I admit it. I skipped pages.

All children should do that.

If they do, they'll be able to enter mysteries supposedly inaccessible to them at their age.

If they have a hankering to read *Moby Dick,* but get discouraged by Melville's discourse about the latest whaling equipment and techniques, they should not give up. Let them skip those pages and follow Ahab as he pursues his great white reason for living and dying. If they want to meet Ivan and Dimitri and Alyosha Karamazov and their incredible father, let them open *The Brothers K.* and start reading. It was written for them, even if they have to skip over the testament of the *starets* Zossima and the Tale of the Grand Inquisitor.

If they don't decide by themselves what's within their understanding by skipping the pages of their choice, someone will do it for them. Someone else will take up the crude scissors of imbecility and snip out everything judged too difficult for them. The results will be dreadful, condensed 150-page versions

of *Moby Dick* and *Les Misérables,* mutilated, trun-
cated, flattened, mummified, rewritten in an impov-
erished language that someone thinks is appropriate
for their level. While we're at it, why not redraw
Picasso's *Guernica,* since the artist put in way too
many lines for the eye of a twelve-year-old?

Even adults, though we'd rather not admit it,
read diagonally once in a while. Why? That's between
us and the book. On the other hand, some of us
refuse to do it and read everything down to the last
word, even as we judge that Author A chewed more
than he bit off, or that Author B flew off into needless
digressions, or that Author C repeated herself, or that
Author D misplaced his sense of judgment. If we're
stubborn and choose boredom, it's not out of a sense
of duty; it's just another pleasure among the many
pleasures of reading.

3.

The Right to Not Finish a Book

There are 36,000 good reasons to put down a novel before its natural end. The feeling that we've read it before. A story that fails to hold our attention. Our total disagreement with the author's main argument. A style that rubs us the wrong way, or an absence of style that keeps us from wanting to know anything more ... That leaves 35,995 other good reasons, including a raging toothache, an intolerant boss, a deafening heart murmur ...

Is the book slowly slipping from our grasp?

Let it go.

After all, we can't all be French philosophers like Montesquieu and automatically derive an hour of comfort from a good book.

But among the reasons for abandoning a book, one gives rise to reflection: the vague feeling of defeat. I open it, I read, and immediately I feel overwhelmed by a force stronger than myself. I marshall my intelligence; I engage in hand-to-hand combat with the book; I do my best, I know that everything written there should be read. But I just don't get it, or I get very little of it. This book offers me no way in.

So I drop it.

Or put it aside. I put it back on the shelf with the vague resolution that one day I'll return. André Biely's *Petersburg,* Joyce's *Ulysses,* Lowry's *Under the Volcano* all had to wait years for me. Others are still waiting; I'll probably never catch up to them. Nothing tragic about it. The notion of maturity in a reader's life is a strange one. When we're young, we're not mature enough for some works, I'll grant you that. But unlike good wine, good books don't age. They wait for us on our shelves while we age. When we fancy ourselves mature enough for them, we give them another chance. Two things can happen: either the encounter is successful, or it's another fiasco. Maybe we'll try again, maybe not. But it's certainly not Thomas Mann's fault if I haven't yet been able to scale the heights of his *Magic Mountain.*

A great novel that keeps us on the outside is not necessarily more difficult than any other. Between its greatness and our ability to understand, a shadow falls. The chemical reaction simply doesn't occur. One day we'll empathize with Borges' work, though it's kept us at a distance for years, whereas we may never reduce the distance between ourselves and Musil.

We have a choice. We can conclude that it's all our fault, that we're a few bricks shy of a load, that deep down we're basically stupid. Or we can appeal to the very controversial notion of taste and begin to explore what our tastes are.

I say we offer the second solution to the young readers in our lives.

It has the advantage of offering the rare pleasure of rereading and understanding *why* they didn't like a certain book. And when some pedantic literature teacher brays, "How can anyone not like Henry James?" they can always give this simple answer.

"There's no accounting for taste."

4.

The Right to Reread

To reread that which once rejected us, to reread every word, to reread in a different light, to reread to check our first impressions: this is one of our rights.

But we can also reread for the hell of it, for the pleasure of repetition, for the happiness of encountering an old friend and putting our friendship to the test once again.

"One more time!" we would say when we were young. As adults, we reread for the same reason. We want the enchantment of an old pleasure that, each time, is rich in new magic.

5.

The Right to Read Anything

When it comes to taste, some of my students have a devil of a time when faced with the standard term-paper subject: "Is There Such a Thing as Good and Bad Novels?" Though they put on a stern face and claim to make no concessions, underneath it all they're accommodating. Instead of looking at the subject as a literary problem, they adopt the ethical point of view and see it as a freedom-of-speech issue. Most of their arguments can be summed up this way: "There's no such thing as good and bad novels. We have the right to write what we want to, and readers have the right to exercise their tastes, too!"

Of course, the position is a completely honorable one.

But there still are good and bad novels. Names can be quoted, proof given.

To make a long story short, let's imagine something called "industrial literature." Its job is to reproduce, *ad infinitum,* the same types of stories, to grind out assembly-line stereotypes, to retail noble sentiments and trembling emotions, to seize every opportunity to turn current events into docu-dramas, to conduct market studies in order to manufacture, according to demographic profile, products designed to tease the imaginations of specific categories of consumers.

That's what I call bad novels.

Why? Because they're not creations. Because they reproduce pre-established forms. Their enterprise is one of simplification (lies, in other words), whereas the novel is the art of truth (complexity, in other words). Because by provoking knee-jerk reactions, they lull our curiosity. Because the author is absent, and so is the reality he or she claims to describe.

This is "heat and serve" literature, the product of a mold we're supposed to fit into, too.

Don't assume that these idiocies are a recent phenomenon, linked to the industrialization of books. On the contrary. Sensationalism, purple prose, facile sentiments in authorless fictions have a long history. The chivalric romance bogged down this way, as did romanticism, centuries later. But since every cloud has a silver lining, the reaction to this denatured literature gave our world two of its finest novels: *Don Quixote* and *Madame Bovary.*

So there *are* "good" and "bad" novels.

We usually run into the latter kind first.

Believe me, when I encountered them for the first time, I figured they were cracking good yarns. I was lucky. No one ever made fun of me, no one lifted his eyes heavenward, no one called me a moron. A few "good" novels were put where I could reach them, and no one censored the other kind.

That was true wisdom.

For a while, we read the good and the bad together, just as we don't turn away from our childhood reading in a single day. Everything coexists. We emerge from *War and Peace* and return to the Hardy

Boys. We go from Harlequin Romances (stories of handsome doctors and deserving nurses) to Boris Pasternak and his *Doctor Zhivago*. Come to think of it, that book had a handsome doctor, too, and his Lara was a very deserving nurse!

Then, one day, Pasternak wins the race. Imperceptibly, we begin to turn towards "good" novels. We search out writers and writing. We want more than playmates; we want to share our being. Anecdote alone does not quench our thirst. We begin to expect a novel to give us something more than the immediate and exclusive gratification of our senses.

This is one of the joys of teaching: though the door to the bestseller factory is open, the student will slam it shut herself and turn to Balzac to breathe in a little fresh, wild air.

6.

The Right to Escapism

Immediate gratification of our senses is what escapism is all about. Our imaginations swell, our nerves jangle, our hearts soar, adrenaline surges, identification goes in search of a port in the storm. For a moment, the brain mistakes the pig's ear of daily life for the silk purse of romance.

As readers, all of us started out that way.

It was wonderful.

Though a bit alarming for the adult observer who would have preferred to put a solemn piece of "great literature" into our hands.

"Here, try some Henry James. You must admit, it's better for you."

Don't panic; don't escape escapism. The French have a word for it. They call it *bovarysme*, after poor Emma of Flaubert's *Madame Bovary,* that celebrated seeker of sensations. But don't forget that Emma Bovary herself is just a character in a novel, the product of the fictional situation that Flaubert created to get the effect—a true effect, mind you—he was after.

In other words, just because a young girl consumes Harlequin Romances doesn't mean she'll end up literally dying for love.

If we cut off the route to escape too quickly, we'll estrange ourselves from young readers and deny our own teenage years in the process. Don't readers first have to explore the world of stereotypes so they can recognize them later?

Our teenage years are important ones. To despise or deny or simply forget the teenager who lives in all of us is in itself an adolescent attitude, one that treats that crucial passage as if it were a disease.

Let's not forget the first waves of emotion that reading brought us. Why not revisit and pay our respects to the books of our youth, including the most escapist of them? They can still play an important role in our lives. We may be moved by what we were and laugh at what once moved us. The teenagers in our lives will love and respect us more for it.

The desire for escapism is something everyone shares, and it's one of those things we always discover in other people first. Even as we mock the rank escapism of much adolescent reading, we're panting after the latest telegenic novelist whom we'll deride once his or her fifteen minutes of fame are up. Literary trends follow the pendulum that swings between infatuation and sober rereading after the first excitement has passed.

We're nobody's fool. We're always clear-headed. Ask us, and we'll tell you that Madame Bovary is the reader next door.

Emma must have held the same opinion.

7.

The Right to Read Anywhere

Châlons-sur-Marne, winter 1971.

The barracks at the Gunnery School.

When it comes to assigning details, Private So-and-So (serial number 14672/1, well known to the service) systematically volunteers for the least desirable, most disgusting detail, the one usually handed out as a punishment, that has tried the bravery of greater men: the legendary, infamous, unnameable latrine detail!

Every morning.

With the same half-smile.

"Who wants latrine detail?"

He steps forward.

"Private So-and-So!"

With a sense of mission, as if he were going off to storm Hamburger Hill, he grabs the mop and pail, his company colors, and marches off, much to the relief of his fellow soldiers. He's a brave man. No one follows him. The rest of the company lies low in the trenches of more honorable details.

The hours go by. Where has he gone? We almost forgot him. We did forget him. But just before noon, he shows up with a salute to the sergeant. "Latrines clean as a whistle, sir!" The sergeant receives the mop and pail. He'd like to ask the question that's on his mind, but basic human respect stops him. Private So-and-So salutes again, turns on his heels and marches off, his secret still intact.

The secret is contained in that thick book in his uniform pocket: the 1,900 pages of Gogol in a paperback college edition. The complete works. Fifteen minutes of noxious detail, and he's free to spend the rest of the morning with Nikolai Gogol. Every morning through the winter, seated comfortably on a throne in a locked stall, Private So-and-So soars far above latrine detail. Nikolai Gogol, down to the last word! From the nostalgic *Evenings on a Farm near*

Dikanka to the uproarious *Petersburg Tales,* with a stop to visit the terrible *Taras Bulba,* and the dark laughter of *Dead Souls,* through to the plays and correspondence of that incredible Tartuffe himself, Nikolai Gogol.

That's Gogol: Tartuffe inventing Molière. Private So-and-So would never have understood that if someone else had drawn that particular detail.

The army likes to celebrate its exploits.

But of this one, only two lines remain, written high up on the edge of the watercloset. They are among the most meaningful in all contemporary poetry:

> *It's no lie when I tell you, pedagogue*
> *That I read all of Gogol in the bog.*

(While we're on the subject, old Georges Clemenceau, AKA "The Tiger," another famous fighter, thanked his chronic constipation, without which, so he said, he would never have had the pleasure of reading Saint-Simon's *Memoirs.*)

8.

The Right to Browse

I browse. We all browse. So let them browse.

Many of us exercise the right to pull any book off the shelf at home, open it at any page and jump right in for the minute or two we have at our disposal. Some books lend themselves to browsing, especially those made of short, separate sections: the complete works of Alphonse Allais and Woody Allen, Kafka's and Saki's stories, Georges Perros' *Papiers collés,* our old friend La Rochefoucauld and most poets.

At the same time, we can pick up Proust or Shakespeare or Raymond Chandler's *Selected Letters* and start reading anywhere, browsing here and there, without risk of disappointment.

If you don't have the time or the means to spend a week in Venice, why turn down a five-minute stay?

9.

The Right to Read Out Loud

I asked her, "Did your parents read to you when you were young?"

"Never," she answered. "My father traveled a lot, and my mother was always too busy."

I asked her, "How did you come to love reading out loud?"

"From school," she answered.

I was so pleased that someone admitted having gotten something out of school that I exclaimed happily, "There! You see?"

"Not at all," she told me. "At school, they forbade us to read out loud. Silent reading was the fashion then. Quiet transition from eye to brain.

Instant transcription, rapid and efficient. With a comprehension test every ten lines. The religion of analysis and commentary was there from the start. Most kids nearly died of fright, and that was only the beginning. I was good at it, as it turned out, but when I got home I reread the whole assignment out loud."

"Why?"

"For the pleasure of hearing it. When I pronounced the words, they began to exist outside of me, they really came alive. For me, it was an act of love. It was love itself. I always thought that the love of books was part of love in general. I tucked my dolls into my bed and read to them. Sometimes I would fall asleep at the foot of the bed, on the rug."

I listened to her. As I did, I felt I was listening to Dylan Thomas, drunk on despair, reading his poems in his cathedral voice.

I listened to her and pictured old Charles Dickens, bony and pale, near death, climbing once more onto the stage. His illiterate audience is entranced. They're so quiet they can hear the pages turn. Oliver Twist ... Nancy's death ... He's going to read us Nancy's death!

I listened to her and heard Kafka laughing

himself silly as he reads his *Metamorphosis* to Max Brod, who's not sure he gets the joke. I see the young Mary Shelley offering passages of her *Frankenstein* to Percy and their terrified friends.

I listened to her, and here comes Martin du Gard reading his *Thibault* to Gide ... but Gide doesn't seem to be taking it in. They're sitting on a riverbank, Martin du Gard is reading, but Gide's eyes are elsewhere. Gide is watching two young boys diving into the river, a little further on ... The water has clothed their perfection in light ... Martin du Gard is mad as hell. But he shouldn't be, he read well, and Gide heard it all, and now he's telling his friend how much he admires his pages, though, still, he might consider changing a thing or two ...

Reading out loud wasn't good enough for Dostoevsky; he had to write out loud, too. Dostoevsky, completely out of breath after shouting out his indictment of Raskolnikov (or was it Dimitri Karamazov, or both?), Dostoevsky, asking Anna Grigorievna, his stenographer spouse, "So? What should it be? What's the verdict? Tell me!"

Anna: "Guilty!"

Then, turning the tables, Dostoevsky dictates the defense's brilliant plea.

"Now what? Now what? What do you say now?"

Anna: "Not Guilty!"

Of course.

How strange that reading out loud has disappeared from our world. What would Dostoevsky make of that? Or Flaubert? Have we lost the right to hear the words from our mouths before we stuff them into our heads? Have we lost our ear? Our sense of music? Has our saliva run dry? Have words lost their taste? Think of it! Didn't Flaubert shout out his *Madame Bovary* until his eardrums bled? Didn't he absolutely, essentially understand, better than anyone else, that the intelligence of his story moved through the sound of his words and from that sound all meaning flowed? He understood that meaning must be spoken, though all through his career he raged against the tempestuous music of syllables and the tyranny of rhythm. Would you impose the silent pages of pure spirits on me? No, sir! Give me Rabelais! Give me Flaubert! Dostoevsky! Kafka!

Dickens! Bring them on! Bellowers of meaning, all larger than life! Come and bring our books to life! Our words need a body! Our books need life!

The mute page is comfortable, I agree. It would certainly spare us Dickens' fate, with his doctors begging him to silence his novels, just this once ... The page and the self, muzzled in the cozy rooms of our intelligence, with commentary working its silent knitting needles! When we judge a book outside ourselves, there's no danger of it judging us. But once the human voice is engaged, the book begins to comment on its reader. The book says it all.

He who reads aloud exposes himself absolutely. If he doesn't understand what he's reading, he betrays himself out loud. It's a shame, and you can hear it. If he's not as one with his book, the words will die on his tongue and leave a taste. If he bullies the book with his voice, the author retreats; the performance becomes a pantomime, and you can see it. He who reads aloud exposes himself to whoever hears him.

If he *really* reads, if he adds all his understanding to the act and masters his pleasure, if his reading becomes an act of empathy with the audience and the book and its author, if he can communicate the necessity of writing by touching our deepest need for stories, then books will open their doors, and those who felt excluded from reading will follow him inside.

10.

The Right to Not Defend Your Tastes

We build houses because we are alive; we write books because we know we're mortal. We live in packs because we're gregarious; we read because we know we're alone. Reading offers companionship that fills no void, yet no other being can take its place. It offers no definitive explanation of our destiny, yet it weaves a tight web of complicity between the world and ourselves. Tiny, secret acts of complicity that speak of the paradoxical joy of living, even as they illuminate the tragic absurdity of life. Our reasons for reading are as eccentric as our reasons for living. No outsider can demand an explanation of that secret intimacy.

Those few adults who gave me the gift of reading let their books speak and never once asked if I had *understood*. Naturally, I went to them when I wanted to talk. Living on this earth or in memory alone, I dedicate these pages to them.

ACKNOWLEDGEMENTS

In Chapter 21, the excerpt from Jean-Jacques Rousseau is taken from *Emile,* translated by Barbara Foxley, Everyman's Library, 1933.

In Chapter 25, the two excerpts from Gustave Flaubert are taken from the Gerard Hopkins translation of *Madame Bovary,* UOP, 1981. The second translation has been slightly modified.

In Chapter 31, the excerpt from Klaus Mann is taken from *The Turning Point,* Serpent's Tail, 1987.

In Chapter 33, the line from Flannery O'Connor is taken from *The Habit of Being,* Farrar, Strauss & Giroux, 1979.

In Chapters 44 and 45, the excerpts from Patrick Süskind are taken from *Perfume,* translated by John E. Woods, Alfred A. Knopf, 1986.

In Chapter 47, the excerpt from Gabriel Garcia Márquez is taken from *One Hundred Years of Solitude,* translated by Gregory Rabassa, Picador, 1978.

Also in Chapter 47, the excerpt from Benjamin Constant is taken from *Adolphe,* translated by Carl Wildman, Curwen Press, 1948.

In Chapter 56, the excerpt by Flannery O'Connor is also taken from *The Habit of Being.*

The translator and the publisher thank Daniel Pennac for his permission to adapt certain aspects of this book.